Revealing the Truth, Exposir

MW00777786

Revealing the Truth, Exposing Injustice, and Trusting God

The
Scott Sisters

Revealing the Truth, Exposing Injustice, and Trusting God

Jamie and Gladys
Scott

Revealing the Truth, Exposing Injustice, and Trusting God

The Scott Sisters:
Revealing the Truth, Exposing Injustice, and Trusting God

Printed in the United States of America

ISBN 978-0692606032
ISBN 0692606033

The Scott Sisters: Revealing the Truth, Exposing Injustice, and Trusting God ~ Copyright © 2015 by Gladys Scott and Jamie Scott

No part of this book may be reproduced or transmitted in any form or by any means, electronic or mechanical, including photocopying, recording, or by any information storage and retrieval system, without permission in writing from the authors. Published in the United States of America.

Cover Art by Kenyatta Jackson-Harvey
Photograph by Abraham Booker

The Scott Sisters

DEDICATION

To Mama & Daddy
(James & Evelyn Rosco)

To all those who have been falsely accused, convicted, and
To those serving time for crimes they did not committ.

The Scott Sisters

Revealing the Truth, Exposing Injustice
and Trusting God

CONTENTS

FOREWORD

"Gladys, I am NOT going to that church!"

   "Why not, Jamie?"

   *"I'm not going to that church because of the pastor. Look
at him. No, look at him! He looks like he's 12 years old! Now,
what can that little boy tell me? I need something! I need
somebody that can teach me and tell me something!"*

   *"Well, pray about it, Jamie, because I think this is where I
am joining."*

   "I ain't joining, Gladys. I'm just not."

   That was the first conversation Jamie and Gladys had
concerning me. Since Gladys was a little ahead of Jamie on
this one, she joined in April of 2011. Jamie eventually visited
enough to see things differently than the way she originally
saw them and she came in January of 2012. But even that
scenario is a great synopsis of the way Jamie and Gladys have
evolved on their personal journey. If you do not get anything
else out of this book, I would hope for you to see how both
Jamie and Gladys have come to appreciate the processes of
life. The way things go. The reasons why things sometimes
might have to go a certain way. Good and bad. And this is not
to say that either of them has given in to believe about
themselves what others say they (and everyone else) should
believe. No, (believe me) it is not.

   They know who they are, and they know what they have
not done. But this is to say that the "Scott Sisters" have come

to grips with the road they have been destined to travel, and they have now embraced that road through the telling of their story - their way. This is to say that both Jamie and Gladys have suffered enough, cried enough, hurt enough, and have seen enough to be able to finally tell their story. They want to tell it to help others who may be incarcerated. They want to tell it to help keep someone from being incarcerated.

By going back to their childhood days of Chicago, Jamie and Gladys show a wonderful appreciation for, and a splendid resolve in, their private experiences. Their love of family is astounding. Their pain of injustice is blinding. Their love of God is reassuring.

Would it be easier to blame everyone else for what they have been through? Of course it would. Their family continues to suffer from it today. Would it have been more lucrative to latch on to someone with dollar signs in their eyes? We all know that answer. But that is not who Jamie and Gladys Scott are. That's not who James and Evelyn Rasco reared them to be.

The process of life for the "Scott Sisters" has them where they are, and they can appreciate that - now. They have grown enough to appreciate that. They are bigger than Haley Barbour. They are bigger than the Scott County justice system. They are bigger than double life sentences. They have seen the process take them from Chicago, Illinois to Sugar Hill in Forest, Mississippi to Pensacola, Florida...on their way to freedom.

Lonnie D. Wesley, III
Pastor
Greater Little Rock Baptist Church
Pensacola, Florida

PREFACE

Finally, we have an opportunity to tell our side of the story...our side of the story regarding the night in question: that one Christmas Eve in 1993, when we allegedly robbed two grown men for eleven dollars. We were advised not to take the stand in court, so now it's our time to talk. We served time for a crime we did *not* commit – armed robbery. Never in our life did we ever think we would end up in prison, and definitely not at nineteen and twenty-one years old, but a chain of ill-fated events topped with one regretful decision handed us a double life prison sentence in the Central Mississippi Correctional Facility in Rankin County, Mississippi.

This book is not just another great story or novel to keep you up at night; this is our life. The pages in this book tell the truth and nothing but the truth about everything that led us to prison and the sixteen years we spent behind bars. We talk about everything from being raised in the projects to the life we live now – on parole. We talk about the challenging times we faced transitioning to the free world, and getting to know the kids we left behind. We share events that happened behind the scenes of our case, and behind the closed doors of our family life. We want you to get to know Jamie and Gladys, not just "The Scott Sisters." This book is literally an open book of our lives.

We're asked all the time, "How did a nineteen and twenty-one-year-old get a double life prison sentence for a crime they didn't commit?" While we sat in prison, we asked ourselves that same question over and over again. There was no evidence in our case. We didn't have prior records. Nobody was hurt, and there was no weapon. Even if we *had* committed the crime, isn't one life sentence enough? We met other inmates in prison who had actually committed crimes worse than ours, but nobody – and we mean *nobody* – was doing the time we were doing. Nobody was serving *two* life sentences.

We were convicted of "Accessory to Armed Robbery," which was later upgraded to "Armed Robbery." We weren't given any explanation as to why the crime was upgraded; it just happened. There were a lot of *whys* in our case that were left unanswered. We made some mistakes in life, and we haven't always made the best decisions, but we did *not* commit armed robbery or any other crime to warrant going to prison. We sure didn't deserve a *double* life sentence. We were wrongly convicted and we will always maintain our innocence. Sharing our story will hopefully answer a lot of questions. We chose to reveal things about ourselves, and our family, that we've never shared before. Knowing a little more about us instead of an introduction from Google or what the media has reported will help you to better understand our bizarre story.

While we were writing this book, some of the things that happened in our childhood brought back painful memories. Some of the experiences we had in prison stirred up a lot of anger and sadness, but we also experienced a lot of healing.

Remembering our past and publicly sharing our lives gave us a chance to get to know a part of ourselves that we've never acknowledged. When this book was finished and we read it for the first time, it was hard to believe that we were really reading about our own lives. What happened to us is unbelievable – even to us.

We co-authored this book, so throughout the book, you'll see certain statements by us separately because even though our life took the same path – which led to prison – we didn't always react the same. Sharing our own thoughts will also help you to get to know us as individuals. We each had our own double life sentence to serve. We each had to deal with experiencing prison life as a young adult. We're sisters, but again, we want you to get to know Jamie Scott and Gladys Scott on a personal level, and not just as the "Scott Sisters."

We will probably be referred to as the "Scott Sisters" for the rest of our lives. We're nationally known and recognized, but it would be nice to be known and recognized for something else besides armed robbery. Being the "Scott Sisters" hasn't been easy. The constant interviews with media and questions from the public, not to mention comments from those who believe we deserved to go to prison, are things we deal with more than we care to mention. We just want to live a normal life, but since we're on parole for the rest of our lives, normal won't be visiting us no time soon. We're free, but we're not functionally free. It's hard to think about the day we were released from prison without thinking about how we got to prison in the first place. Our trial was the most bizarre trial we've ever heard of, and the fact that it was actually *our* trial,

3

Jamie and Gladys Scott, makes it that much more bizarre to us.

Everybody has a right to their opinion, and we hope after reading our story and the facts behind our case, your verdict will be accurate. We are, without a doubt, innocent. This is our life; and it is the truth, the whole truth, and nothing but the truth.

THE KNOCK

Christmas Eve was always an extra special holiday in our family because it was also our Daddy's birthday. We always looked forward to the double-celebration and spending that day with close friends and family. On December 24th 1993, at approximately 9:00 a.m., there was a knock at the door that changed our lives forever. We will never forget that disturbing morning knock that set off our family nightmare.

Every year, Mama planned a big dinner party for the family's double-celebration. Mama would start cooking three days before the party, and would have tables full of food and everybody would come and eat, drink, and have a good ole' time. Mama cooked some of our favorite dishes like chitlins, cornbread dressing, and macaroni-and-cheese. Nobody could make homemade macaroni-and-cheese like Mama. We remember it being so creamy and cheesy; it was the best. Mama had us in the kitchen helping her, and everybody had an assignment. We didn't mind because the smell of Mama's Southern country cooking filled the whole house and had everybody anxious to fix a plate. Christmas Eve was a fun time of year that we always looked forward to. Unfortunately, instead of being served Mama's meal, we were being served a warrant for our arrest.

Jamie

I was relaxing on the sofa with my two-year-old son. I was recovering from having my tubes tied, so I was supposed to be taking it easy. I heard a knock at my door. I didn't feel like getting up to answer it, but I did. When I opened the door, I was shocked to see three sheriffs standing on the porch and three patrol cars parked in the yard. My heart started beating real fast, and the first thing I did was try to place the whereabouts of my family members in my head. I didn't feel like hearing no bad news, especially on Christmas Eve. The three sheriffs invited themselves in, and one said they had a warrant for me and Gladys' arrest. The charge was "Accessory to Armed Robbery." I laughed. I literally laughed out loud at the officer. I knew it had to be a sick joke or a mistake. When the sheriffs showed no signs of their official visit being comical, I yelled out for Gladys.

Gladys

I was in the back room, and heard Jamie yell out my name to come up front. I could tell by the way she yelled my name that somethin' was wrong, so I stopped what I was doin' and went up front where she was. When I walked in the room and saw the three sheriffs standin' at the door, I knew it couldn't be nothin' but some bad news. I braced myself to hear that somebody was in a accident, or maybe somebody had died. When Jamie told me the reason for the sheriffs' visit, I understood why she was lookin' so crazy and confused - she looked like she was in shock. I was just as shocked, and my heart started beatin' faster than I ever felt it beat before. *What the hell?*

6

~

The three officers were serious and didn't want to entertain our questions, but we were just as serious. We fired questions at them left and right without giving them time to answer: "Are you out of your damn mind?" "What are you talking about?" "Robbed who?" "When did we rob somebody?"

Unfortunately, we had more questions than they had answers. We only received underhanded, snide smiles and handcuffs from one of the officers. We had absolutely no intentions of letting them handcuff us, and we definitely weren't leaving with the officers because we hadn't done nothing wrong. The sheriffs tried to put handcuffs on us, but we weren't about to let that happen. We weren't leaving the house – period. Resisting arrest wasn't on our minds, and we resisted with everything we had. If we had to leave, we weren't going to leave without a fight – and boy did we fight. We fought with every fiber in our bodies like trapped wild animals fighting to get free. We fought with strength we didn't know we had and as if our life depended on it. As it turns out, our life *did* depend on it.

It was a good thing we lived on Daddy's property because he could hear and see everything that went on with us. Daddy always kept us close to him, so he could always be there when we needed him. Even when we were little girls, Daddy tried his best to always keep an eye on us, and when he was working, he made sure Mama knew where we were all the time. From his house, Daddy saw the three patrol cars in the yard and heard the commotion coming from the house. He panicked, hurriedly ran over, and burst through the front door while we were tussling with the officers. Mama wasn't far behind. Daddy came just in time to prevent the situation from getting out of hand. Daddy, as he always did, came to our rescue. Panicked and pissed, Daddy was able to somewhat calm us down long enough to ask the officers questions and find out what was going on. Daddy didn't get any answers either. So, devastated and confused, we reluctantly agreed to leave with the sheriffs.

Daddy said everything would get straightened out at the sheriff's office, and we believed him. Daddy always found his way out of trouble, and we trusted him to take care of this obvious false arrest, which was, without a doubt in our minds, a big mistake. Daddy was always right, so we didn't feel like we had nothing to worry about. Nevertheless, we were handcuffed and the three officers led us to the front door. Our kids were crying and calling out for us, so Mama got them together and tried her best to quiet them down. They saw everything that happened between us and the officers. Mama couldn't comfort them or calm them down. They just kept crying uncontrollably. We didn't blame them. Their young eyes didn't understand what was going on. We didn't understand what was going on either, but we sure weren't crying about it. We were too pissed to cry.

Our kids watched us walk out of the house, handcuffed, and as we were escorted to the patrol cars, we heard them crying out: "I want my mama!" "Mama!" "Mama come back!"

Hearing their sad voices calling out for us ripped our hearts apart. We felt hopeless, but we weren't the only ones feeling hopeless. The look on Mama's face showed she *desperately* wanted to do more, but she couldn't. At that point, there was nothing that nobody could do. As she held onto her crying grandchildren, Mama watched her own children being taken away in handcuffs. Our Christmas Eve celebration went from cheerful to complete confusion. We were put in separate patrol cars and taken away.

Jamie

Looking through the back window of the patrol car, I saw my kids crying and trying to pull away from Mama, who was doing her best to hold them back. My two-year-old, Terrance, somehow broke away from Mama's grip, and ran towards the patrol car as fast as his little chubby legs would let him. He didn't get too far before Mama pulled him back. I had to look away because it was too heartbreaking to watch. I wanted to break out of those handcuffs and get my baby boy. I looked forward and there was a bar in front of me that separated the back seat from the front seat. I couldn't believe I was actually riding in the back seat of a sheriff's car. *Me?*

Gladys

I was mad as hell and out of breath from fightin'. I wanted to fight some more, but I knew Daddy would take care of us. I was wonderin' if Jamie was okay since she had just had surgery. She was s'posed to be takin' it easy, but instead she was fightin' hard like she was fightin' for her life. We were in separate cars but we felt each other's fear and confusion. It didn't seem real. We ain't never been in trouble with the law before. Armed robbery? It didn't make no sense to me.

~

The ride to the sheriff's office gave us time to catch our breath, but we were still mad and confused. We hadn't robbed anybody and didn't have a clue what the sheriffs were talking about, but we were about to find out. We knew we would be home in time to enjoy the family celebration, and especially mama's mouth-watering Christmas dinner that she slaved over. Mama worked too hard on that meal for it to be ruined by nonsense. We had planned to entertain close friends and family on Christmas Eve, but instead we were getting ready to entertain a line of questioning from the sheriff's department. Once we got to the station, we were escorted inside and read our rights.

We couldn't wait for Daddy to get to the sheriff's office. Our hometown was small, but we remember the drive to the Scott County Sheriff's Department taking forever, and it seemed like it was taking Daddy forever to get there, too. Sheriff Marvin Williams and Sheriff Jerry McNeese were the names of the two officers asking us questions. They vaguely informed us of two young men who were also charged in the same, so-called robbery. We knew the two men from around town, but our arrest still didn't make any sense to us. We were so confused. Armed robbery?

The questioning then took an odd turn to questions about

our father. The officers all of a sudden seemed more interested in our father's business and social circle than our alleged armed robbery. They wanted to know more about Daddy's life and who he knew and didn't know. Daddy finally got to the station, and we were relieved to see his face. He came to rescue us. The fear and anxiety that had built up in us from all the questions disappeared as soon as we saw Daddy's face. Just knowing Daddy came to straighten things out and take us home made us calm down. Daddy looked pissed, like he was ready to beat the hell outta somebody. Nobody messes with Daddy's girls.

Jamie

As soon as I saw Daddy, I yelled out, "Daddy, they wanna know about you!" Daddy yelled, "So, this how y'all wanna play?" We didn't understand Daddy's statement, nor did we understand all the yelling going on between him and the sheriffs. We heard Daddy say, "Y'all tryin' to frame my daughters 'cause I won't play ball wit' y'all?" Daddy was pissed and we were more confused.

The sheriffs told us if we gave them the names of Daddy's connections, they would let us out and we would be home in time to open Christmas presents with our kids. We may have been young and confused at the time, but we knew a bribe when we heard one. We didn't know nothing about any "connections," so we couldn't offer no information. After a while, Daddy just stood in front of the officers looking stone-faced and defenseless. That was the first time we ever saw

11

Daddy look completely helpless, and his look scared us. But even with the powerless look on his face, he kept assuring us that he would get everything taken care of, and we believed him. In the meantime, we were placed in separate jail cells.

Gladys

I was put in a holdin' cell by myself. I cussed a lot and refused to cooperate. I was pissed off, and woulda fought anybody in my way. I knew Jamie was glad I was in a cell by myself, so I wouldn't stir up more mess. Jamie was in a cell with some other folks. She was bein' real quiet. I know she was in shock. I was in shock, too, but sho' wasn't tryin' to be quiet.

~

We wondered what Daddy meant by his strange comments to the sheriffs. Framed? Were we being framed? Framed for what? Was Daddy involved in something we didn't know about? We knew Daddy had to have some kinda connections back during the days when he owned a night club. He had to know somebody who would let him buy his liquor, because it was against the law to sell liquor in Scott County...but we knew there was no way we spent sixteen years in prison over no liquor. Daddy never told us how he got anything done, and he sure didn't share what was going on behind-the-scenes. Daddy didn't even tell Mama nothing. We all just reaped the benefits of Daddy's hustle and hard work. While we sat in jail, we thought long and hard about the Sugar Hill days.

Lookin' Back

Daddy's nephew used to own a night club called "Sugar Hill" in Forest, Mississippi. His nephew was involved in some type of investigation with the FBI, so the club had to be shut down because of it. Daddy's nephew had knowledge of a local sheriff being paid off by the town's black club-owners to allow the sale of alcohol in their clubs. Because the investigation led to the imprisonment of that sheriff, Daddy's nephew entered the witness protection program, which meant Sugar Hill had to shut down. We had just moved to Forest, Mississippi from Chicago and Daddy was looking for work. Daddy saw dollar bills on the closed Sugar Hill establishment, and even though he didn't have no experience running a club or any other type of business, Daddy knew how to make a dollar work for him.

Daddy never learned to read or write, and could hardly write his name, but he didn't doubt that he could make good money reopening Sugar Hill, so he did. Daddy was always a good provider, but we knew Forest, Mississippi was going to be a challenge for him. There were way more job opportunities in Chicago. Daddy didn't have book smarts, but he was smart about the dollar bill – real smart. Daddy's mom told us he came from a long-line of family members who came up with illegal money-making ideas. We had hoped Daddy would find a good, decent job, like his job at the hospital in Chicago, but Sugar Hill was calling his name – and he answered.

One way or another, our dad, James Rasco, was going to provide for and protect his family like he always did. Mama didn't have much to say about Daddy re-opening Sugar Hill, but she really didn't like the idea of it. She didn't like the idea of Daddy running a club that already had a bad rap. She supported Daddy anyway because she knew Daddy needed to do what he had to do to make a living and support the family.

Daddy knew a night club had to have women and liquor, so he made it happen. He found a few females to strip in Sugar Hill, and the men rolled in and brought their dollar bills with them. Daddy knew liquor would bring more money into Sugar Hill, but the sale of liquor was illegal in Scott County. Daddy wasn't about to run a night club without liquor. So again, Daddy did what he needed to do. Daddy obviously knew the right people, because liquor never ran out in Sugar Hill. He didn't keep the liquor bottles in the club. He hid them in the back of the club, deep in the woods. Liquor and strippers made Sugar Hill an overnight success – literally. We never knew how Daddy brought everything together, but he worked his money-making magic.

In no time, Sugar Hill went from a closed, abandoned building to a standing-room-only, booming night club. Everything happened so fast. Daddy meant business; he always did. He knew how to talk and who to talk to to make things happen. Daddy knew how to make a dollar, and he knew how to make a dollar multiply. The dollars were rolling into Sugar Hill quicker than we could count them. Forest, Mississippi was a small, country town and had never had anything like Sugar Hill before. The town folks had never experienced the entertainment and excitement they saw in Sugar Hill. So whenever a new customer came, they were sure to tell somebody else.

There were other clubs in Forest, but not like Sugar Hill. Daddy's night club was jam-packed and jumpin' every weekend, and it only cost three dollars to get in. Word traveled far and fast about Sugar Hill, and the people kept coming. As the crowd grew, so did the frequency of sheriffs' cars driving by. The patrol cars made Sugar Hill customers uncomfortable, but not uncomfortable enough to leave. The people kept coming – the regulars and new ones who were curious about all the talk of the new place in town. Sugar Hill was the place to be. It was Forest's new hot spot. Unfortunately, the hot spot was heating up jealousy and envy, too.

Daddy's behind-the-scene connections led to a few special requests from some high-powered officials in Scott County. These officials wanted a piece of Daddy's profits...they wanted a *cut*. Daddy refused to share a dollar of his hard-earned money, which must've been the wrong answer because the sheriffs' cars were driving by even more, and it was obvious that the hot spot's success wasn't received well by certain county officials. It didn't look good for the new guy in town to come and take over. Everybody knew Daddy, and knew he was making money. Daddy was making *big* money, and this didn't settle well with county officials.

At first, we thought maybe the sheriffs were keeping an eye on Sugar Hill because they thought Daddy was doing something illegal, or maybe since Sugar Hill got to be so popular and successful so fast, they thought Daddy needed extra protection. After awhile, we realized they thought Daddy was just up to no good, and was waiting for him to make a bad move. We didn't really know what to think. Mama would complain about being followed around town, and she started to feel uncomfortable about the whole Sugar Hill environment. Mama thought the county officials were upset 'cause Daddy was making so much money, and wouldn't share his profits. Daddy didn't care, and just kept doing what he did best – making money.

Daddy eventually needed more help running Sugar Hill, and since our older sister was already working there, Daddy decided to let us work there, too – but he made sure we stayed far away from the liquor. We cooked hamburgers, fried fish, and we barbequed ribs. The crowd couldn't resist the sweet smell of the perfectly-seasoned peppers and onions that we cut up and grilled. We served hot French fries and baked beans on the side. The meals alone brought in a lot of money, but it wasn't enough money for Daddy. Daddy took advantage of every chance he got to make another dollar.

Even when the club closed at night, the poker players would come out and a whole new crowd would fill Sugar Hill. The poker games lasted until the wee hours of the morning and then another new crowd would come – the chicken catchers. They were called chicken catchers because that's exactly what they did, they caught chickens. The local chicken plant brought Sugar Hill a bunch of business. Some of the chicken catchers would come straight off the chicken bus stankin' and tired. They stopped at Sugar Hill to drink

16

whiskey and unwind before going home. Daddy called 'em "old cats." They would put quarters in the juke box and just sit around shooting the breeze and drinking.

There was never a dull moment in Forest, Mississippi's hot spot. The few hours Sugar Hill was closed, people would sit in the parking lot and talk for hours. Sugar Hill was the meeting place – open or closed. Daddy spent a lot of time in Sugar Hill and Mama didn't mind because she liked spending Sugar Hill's money. She never got full control of the money like she wanted, and she didn't try to control her spending habit either.

As the club grew more and more popular, it started attracting all kinds of folks from all over. We saw with our own eyes how running a night club could be dangerous. Some folks came to start trouble, and some came trying to hide from trouble. .Daddy was always breaking up fights. One time, Daddy had to stand between two men fighting, and one had a shot gun. Men would show up at the club with one woman and not know another woman they were seeing was already at the club. Daddy had to break those fights up, too. It was always some mess going on, and we started to fear for Daddy's life. Because of all the commotion that was going on in the club, there seemed to be more patrol cars driving by, but we were used to it. We knew the patrol cars weren't for our protection. We didn't believe for a minute that they were looking out for us, but instead they were looking for something on Daddy. Everybody wasn't happy about Daddy's success, and they let it be known.

One night, the Sheriff's Department raided Sugar Hill for

no reason. Daddy just happened to be in the back of the club, in the woods, getting more whiskey. So when the officers burst in, they were surprised that Daddy wasn't there. Since they couldn't arrest Daddy, they arrested a few of the workers, The whole time this was happening, Daddy was in the woods peeking from behind a tree and watching everything that was going on. He wasn't going to come out of the woods until they left, but one of the sheriffs hit our older sister in the head with his flashlight, and Daddy came running out the woods like a mad man. Daddy was cussin' and going off. The sheriffs must've known Daddy was in the woods, and they knew what would bring him out. Everybody in Forest knew not to mess with Daddy's girls. Daddy would do whatever was necessary to protect his family.

The next day, Mama bailed everybody out and we never heard about that night again. By watching Daddy wheel and deal his way out of trouble, we lost faith in the law and realized money could buy your way out of anything, and we mean anything. Everything has a price. We sat in jail wondering if we had a price, and if we did, why it wasn't paid to keep us out of jail.

That incident didn't slow Daddy down. The money kept rolling in and Daddy started getting smart about how he spent it. He started investing in land. He didn't know a thing about real estate, but he knew the value and benefits of owning a piece of land. He also came up with the bizarre idea to start a women's and men's baseball team. Night life wasn't enough for Daddy, and before we knew it, Daddy owned a baseball field and two teams. We were so proud of him. The word spread like a fire out of control, and out of control is exactly what happened to Daddy. Sugar Hill was soon becoming a 24/7 establishment, and that's where most of his time was spent.

Sugar Hill's crowd grew out of control, and people were coming from places we'd never heard of. Some of these people also brought requests for drugs. Daddy only smoked cigarettes, but Mama smoked a joint everyday – it was her second cigarette. She smoked and got high in front of us like she was smoking cigarettes. Drug use in our family shouldn't have come as a surprise since we grew up around it. Daddy never allowed drug dealing *in* Sugar Hill, but he didn't care what they did *outside* the club, and it wasn't long before Sugar Hill started providing more than excitement and entertainment. Sugar Hill's environment changed, and so did the environment of the quiet, small town of Forest, Mississippi. That wasn't all that changed, Daddy changed, too. It seemed like making money was his main purpose in life. Daddy far exceeded providing for his family. He was feeding his addiction to making money.

We had a lot of time to think about those Sugar Hill days while we sat in jail. A few thoughts brought a half smile to our faces, but most of our thoughts were disturbing thoughts of how we ended up in prison and why. The Sugar Hill days just about convinced us that Daddy's lifestyle had a lot to do with leading us to prison, but we couldn't figure out why we were in prison, and not Daddy.

We did not commit armed robbery, or any other crime for that matter. We hadn't done nothing wrong, but Daddy lived

19

on the edge and gambled with his life and his family by the choices he made. Daddy made a lot of money in those days, but he also made some choices that he probably ended up regretting. Thinking about those days while we sat behind bars didn't solve anything, and only brought more confusion about our living nightmare. We were so confused. We stayed confused with our unanswered questions.

Still in Jail

Christmas morning came, and to our disbelief, we were still sitting in the county jail. We didn't really sleep because we kept waiting on the cell doors to open and for the sheriffs to say we could leave. At ages eighteen and twenty, we were beyond scared. We had never been in trouble before, but we were sitting in the county jail. We kept wondering what was going on and we got more disturbed as the minutes slowly ticked away. Time seemed like it was standing still.

We couldn't believe it. We were in jail on Christmas Day. *Dear God, what in hell is going on?* We thought about our children and what they were doing. We thought about our siblings and wondered what they might be thinking. We thought about our parents and wondered if they really believed in our innocence. We thought spending Christmas Eve in jail was bad, but when our Christmas Eve turned into fourteen days, we thought we were going to lose our minds. It was so unreal to us. We were in prison for armed robbery – for *only* eleven dollars.

On January 7, 1994, Daddy finally bailed us out by using

his land and house as collateral. Daddy didn't want to use cash money because he didn't want nobody to know he had it. We spent almost two weeks in the county jail – two whole weeks! It was pure torture for us, and we knew that would be the first and last time we would ever be in jail. Quite a few family members doubted our innocence in the crime, but as long as our parents believed us, we didn't care what nobody else thought. Daddy found the best lawyers he could and they assured us that everything would be worked out. They convinced us not to worry. We were relieved and thankful to know everything would be taken care of, so we went back to our everyday life. We both had jobs at the local chicken plant cutting up chicken tenders, so every day, we went to work, then went home to take care of our kids.

Daddy picked our trial lawyer, a lawyer who had helped him with one of his previous drug charges. This particular lawyer had Daddy's drug charges dropped by speaking a few words to the Scott County District Attorney and the judge. Daddy wanted us to have only the best representation and he felt confident with his choice. We had no doubt that Daddy knew what he was doing, and we were so thankful to know he would do whatever was necessary to make sure our names were clear of the false arrest.

Having the best representation in court was our opportunity to prove our innocence, so we needed to be prepared and ready without error. We didn't know what to prepare or how to be ready besides just showing up in court with our word that we were innocent, so we left it up to the lawyers. Daddy was expecting our lawyer to make the false charges go away, and so were we. Daddy never went to jail for nothing, so we knew we really didn't have anything to worry about. With every step in the whole accusation mess leading up to our court date, we had to find new hope that we would be free of the false charges. We waited for our court appearance and looked forward to getting the ridiculous charge of "Armed Robbery" behind us and moving forward with our lives.

It seemed to take an eternity, but we finally received a phone call from our lawyer. We hadn't heard anything, so knowing they hadn't forgotten about us felt good. Unfortunately, what they had to say didn't feel good or sound good. Our lawyer said something about a plea bargain. We didn't know what that meant, but after he explained what the term meant, we knew we weren't bargaining for nothing. We were offered a plea bargain for fifteen mandatory years. There was no way we were going to accept a plea bargain; we had no reason to! We did *not* commit the crime, so we had no intentions of doing any more time behind bars. Two weeks in the county jail was more than enough for us. We were innocent, so we weren't bargaining for nothing!

We were indicted in May, six months after our arrest, and our charge of "Accessory to Armed Robbery" was upgraded to "Armed Robbery." We weren't given a reason for the upgrade. There was absolutely no explanation at all – it just happened. Nobody seemed to fight it or do anything about it, so again, we just had to trust that our lawyer knew what he was doing. We were ignorant to the court system and all the language our lawyer used, but we listened real good. We didn't know what questions to ask, so we didn't ask any. We just trusted Daddy to take care of us.

Gladys

Growin' up, I always wanted to be a lawyer. I was good at talkin' in front of people. I ain't never been shy and I love to argue my case or anybody else's case. I would watch courtroom movies like *Perry Mason* all the time. Perry Mason never lost a case; that man *never* lost a case! I knew I could do what Perry Mason did, but instead of bein' a lawyer, I needed a lawyer – a criminal lawyer. Me or Jamie ain't never been in trouble with the law before, and we didn't have no record. I couldn't even wrap my head 'round what was goin' on with us. Me and Jamie always wondered if prison was our destiny 'cause of how we was raised.

PROJECTS TO PRISON

We spent most of our childhood in the projects of Chicago, Illinois where there was never a dull moment. There was always something going on in the projects, just like Sugar Hill. We saw robberies, killings, and we've seen a lot of fights with our own eyes, but that don't make us guilty of nothing. If someone had told us we would end up in prison one day, we would've looked them dead in the face like they were crazy and said, "Yeah, right." Ain't no way in the world were we going to nobody's prison! We were young girls and we had plans for our lives. We had dreams to do something with our life just like any other young person growing up would.

Before we moved to the projects, Mama rented a little, raggedy basement in the slums of Chicago. We remember going down a lot of steps and the basement being dark and dingy. Our three brothers were all crammed up in one small bed together and our older sister and us crammed up together in another bed. That basement was the worst place we ever lived. It was always easier for Mama to find a place for us to live. Daddy was so prideful and didn't like asking for help, so Mama did what she had to do to get her family outta that basement. When it came to her children, Mama always found a way. Mama never had a problem stepping up and speaking up when it came to her children. Mama decided to apply for housing. She refused to settle for that dingy basement, and we remember the day she applied like it was yesterday.

Daddy had an old Cadillac, and all six of us kids stayed in the car with Daddy while Mama was inside this big building fighting for a new place for her family to live. We didn't know what she was doing then, but we found out later that all that time she spent in the building was spent doing paperwork for our new home. Mama must've known she was gonna be awhile because she packed juice, two loaves of bread, and some lunchmeat for us.

Mama was right; she was in that building a real long time, but we just patiently sat in the car with Daddy and ate sandwiches. We had food and Daddy's Blues CD that he played all the time, so we were fine. After a while, Mama walked out of the building and we were happy to see her. She seemed happy, too. She got approved for housing, and we moved from the basement to the 15th floor of the projects. We were moving on up! We were so happy to get out of that dingy basement. The projects was a big step up from that basement and we were proud of Mama for finding a better place for us to live. We don't know how long we would've been in that dingy basement if Mama hadn't taken the initiative to find another place. Mama didn't tip-toe around Daddy's pride, she did what she had to do.

The projects was like new life to us after being in the basement without windows for so long. We went from looking at dingy walls to looking out the window from the fifteenth floor, where there was always something going on. Fussing, fighting, shooting, killing, gang banging...there was always something for us to see and talk about. It was a big difference from the basement.

Daddy tried his best to keep us away from all the action on the streets, but we were curious, and we wanted to see everything in our sight. Unfortunately, Daddy wanted us within *his* sight, so he only let us go as far as right outside our front door. We were forbidden to go any further, so that's where we played – right outside the front door, and not a step further. When Daddy spoke we listened, so we were forced to find ways to have fun in our small, play spot. Mama never had to yell for us to come home 'cause we were already at home – right outside the front door. Mama bought us some chalk, and we would draw and play hopscotch or jump rope. If some of the other kids on the fifteenth floor came out, we would play with them, too. We were always happy to see any other kids we could play with.

When we got tired of playing in front of our door, we would play in our room or look out our bedroom window at everybody else that was outside having fun. We saw a little bit of everything. There were always a bunch of people just standing around, children running around and playing tag or playing in the water from the fire hydrant. We saw people fighting, sitting around laughing, and some just sitting around holding a can or a bottle. It might not sound like much was going on, but it was more going on outside than it was inside, and we wanted to be a part of it.

We wanted to be outside running around with the other kids. They always looked and sounded like they were having so much fun. Sometimes we got so mad being cooped up in the house that we would fill balloons up with water and drop them from our bedroom window. We   would watch who the balloon hit, then laugh and duck down, so they wouldn't see us. We were either bored to death or mad because we weren't outside having fun with everybody else.

We had fun watching the innocent bystanders' reactions when the water balloons hit the ground. We laughed and laughed, and nobody ever figured out where those water balloons were coming from. They would just look up and point. It was like watching our own candid camera show. Mama hardly ever came in our room unless she was coming in to clean, so she never had any idea what we were doing. We had so much fun making our own fun, and it made us forget that we were cooped up in the house. We were kids and we just wanted to have some fun.

We had some good times from that 15th floor bedroom window. We always found something to laugh about. We laughed at a lot of things we probably shouldn't have, but as kids, everybody and everything was funny to us. To this day, we love laughing together. The thought of going to prison *never* crossed our minds while we bombed the sidewalk with water balloons, but a lot of people who followed our case said we were destined to go to prison because of the things we did in our childhood. We were just young and having fun.

Jamie

I dealt with being closed up in our bedroom better than Gladys did, and it was the same way in prison. Gladys didn't deal with being locked up behind bars very well at all. She had a real hard time in prison because there was nowhere for her to go. The fun we shared from our bedroom wasn't enough for Gladys because she never liked being cooped up. As a matter of fact, she hated it. She liked getting out and exploring her surroundings, but there wasn't much for us to explore being surrounded by our four bedroom walls. Gladys was always looking for something to get into.

We were about nine or ten years old before we could finally leave our little play spot at the front door. It didn't matter if Daddy made us stay close to the house or not, we witnessed a depressing lifestyle in the projects every day. We saw and heard a lot of things children shouldn't have to see or hear. Before long, we didn't just witness life in the projects, we started experiencing life in the projects, and before we knew it, we *became* the projects. One by one, our brothers and sisters were touched by either drugs or some type of delinquency. None of our siblings ended up in prison except us.

We're the youngest of our siblings. Mama was married before and had the three boys from her first marriage. Before her divorce was final from her first husband, she met Daddy and they had three girls together–our older sister, Evelyn, and us. This explains why we have a different last name from our mom and dad. People always ask us why our last name is different from our parents' name. If they don't ask, we know they're probably wondering. Mama was still legally married to her first husband, whose last name was Scott, when she had us with Daddy. They never changed our last name, and we never asked why.

Evelyn, our only sister, was named after Mama. Evelyn's nickname was "Boonanie." We called her Boonanie because she was always scared of the Boogieman. Boonanie was the comedian of the family and was always cracking jokes. She kept everybody laughing, and was the life of every party. Boonanie knew how to light up a room, but being funny wasn't her only talent. That girl could sang! Boonanie had a beautiful voice and was *always* around the house hummin' a tune. She sang all the time and didn't hesitate to open her mouth when somebody asked her to sing. We never got tired of listening to Boonanie sing – her voice was just that beautiful.

Our oldest brother, Willie Scott, was nicknamed "Rat" because Mama said he looked like a rat when he was born. Rat always seemed to be secretly ashamed of our family being poor and living in the projects. Rat never liked drama and there was always drama going on in the projects – either outside in the streets or right in our own house. Because Rat was the oldest, he had to watch the rest of us when Mama and Daddy was gone. Rat didn't like having to stay home to babysit us. He always wanted more for his life and wanted to be more, so as soon as he turned eighteen, and not a day later, Rat joined the United States Army.

Rat didn't come around much when he was on leave, and he didn't call much either. Rat got a taste of a better life in the military and probably wanted to forget his life in the projects. When we went to prison, Rat alienated himself even more. Having two sisters in prison for armed robbery probably made him more embarrassed, but we'll be grateful for the few times Rat came to see us while we were incarcerated. Rat wanted to forget about the projects, but he didn't forget about us.

The second-oldest boy is Frederick, nicknamed "Bud." Bud was always a mama's boy. He would stop whatever he was doing to help Mama. As a child, Bud was always running to Mama and whining about anything and everything. We got sick of Bud acting like a big baby. He always wanted to be under Mama. When Mama called, Bud would answer Mama's call in a heartbeat and wouldn't give nobody else a chance to get to her first. Bud was a big help to us when we sat behind bars. For sixteen years, he sent Mama money to help take care of our kids. "Uncle Bud" is what our kids call him. Bud was a blessing to us and our kids.

Terrance is the baby of the boys; we call him "Terry." We're younger than Terry, but we still call him our baby brother. Terry was the first of the six of us to be influenced by all the drugs and crime of the Chicago projects. Our baby brother started getting in trouble when he was real young. He was in and out of jail from the age of twelve. We thought it would stop when he got older, but it just got worse. He kept hanging with the wrong crowds and he stayed in trouble. Terry was under a lot of peer pressure to join a gang and he eventually gave in to the pressure and joined one. It wasn't long before our family was dodging bullets and watching our backs all the time. Terry was respected big time in the streets and rival gangs were always recruiting him, which caused trouble for the rest of the family. We felt like we had to watch our backs and dodge bullets all the time.

Mama was always worried about Terry. It was hard for her to rest when he was out late at night. She would be so relieved when he came home safely; we were all relieved. It didn't matter what time he came home,

Mama was just relieved to see he was alive and safe. We all worried about Terry being a gang member and we knew the drugs would soon follow. There was nothing we could do except hope and pray that Terry would be alright, but Terry wasn't the only one we were hoping and praying for... Boonanie got hooked on drugs, too.

An older guy Boonanie was seeing introduced our big sister to drugs. She didn't sing and crack jokes all the time like she used to, but she was still Boonanie– Boonanie on drugs. We didn't know what to think, watching our brother and sister fall into the lifestyle of the Chicago streets. What was once foreign to us, drugs and crime, became a normal part of our family. We remember seeing drug pushers and users from our 15th floor bedroom window and now they were in the same house with us. It was sad for us to see. With all the drugs around us, you would think we would've been sent to prison for selling drugs instead of armed robbery.

Mama and Daddy didn't want to see their baby girls follow behind Boonanie and Terry, but the streets of Chicago seemed to be snatching our family away one by one. Mama and Daddy tried their best to shelter us, but the more they tried to protect us, the more we wanted to get in the streets. We wanted to see what they didn't want us to see. We saw some of it from our bedroom window, but seeing everything close up was more exciting to us. Mama and Daddy could only protect us so much. When we were finally allowed to play outside instead of in front of the door, Mama and Daddy made sure we stuck together. We had to go everywhere together, and we did. We stuck together like glue. The streets of Chicago made our sisterhood tighter than ever. We walked the streets together, we explored together, and if we needed to, we fought together. Together we also made Mama and Daddy's biggest fear become a reality...we joined a gang. We joined the sister gang our brother, Terry, was a member of. Because Terry got so much respect on the streets, we wanted some of that respect too, but we learned real quick that a gang wasn't the right road to respect.

Our gang didn't seem like a real gang, but seemed more like a bunch of girls who wanted to copy off the male gangs. Our gang bullied people, snatched purses, and fought over project territory. The other gang members never seemed to care about us at all. The only thing they cared about was what we could do for them. They always wanted to see how much trouble we'd get into for the sake of the gang. Our loyalty was supposed to be to each other, as sisters, but it seemed like our loyalty to the gang was always being tested. We never got that respect our brother Terry got, but we felt grown knowing we were in a gang. After so many years of playing at our front door play spot, we were happy to be free, and we made up for all that time we spent looking out the window.

Being in a gang wasn't something we really wanted to do, but it was something to occupy our time. We saw our brother doing it, and other kids doing it, so it seemed like it was the thing to do. And we were having fun...at least we *thought* we were having fun. We were known for not being able to leave our front porch for so long, so joining a gang was our way of showing everybody that we were grown. We knew good and well we didn't have no business being in a gang. Daddy would've had a fit if he found out.

We tried to keep being in a gang a secret from Mama and Daddy, but our brother, Bud, found out. Bud was in the right place at the right time to witness a street fight with a bunch of girls and recognized us in the pile up. We could've been hurt in that pile up, but Bud saved us. Saving us wasn't the only thing Bud did. He told on us, too. He told Mama and Daddy about the gang and, of course, they were mad and made us get out of the gang.

Well, the bad thing about being in a gang was that it was a lot easier to get in than it was to get out. You don't just walk away from a gang. It wasn't easy for us to break loose, so we stayed – we didn't have a choice. We didn't whisper a word about staying in the gang, and nobody knew - not even Bud. We wanted to leave the gang, and Daddy's orders for us to get out was our chance to leave, but the gang didn't take orders, they *gave* orders. We don't think anybody really *wants* to be in a gang, but once you're in, it's not so easy to get out. The gang tried to brainwash us, and make us feel like we had no family but them, but we knew better. The gang was our family as long as we agreed to participate in their gang activity, or until we were ready to walk away.

Gladys

Growin' up together in the Chicago projects brought us closer and closer as sisters, and we depended on our strong bond in prison. When we started gettin' to know other inmates and makin' friends, we remembered everything Daddy taught us 'bout blood bein' thicker than water. Daddy taught us how important family was, and we remembered that in prison – even though prison inmates eventually became our family.

Me and Jamie was best friends. When we was kids, if you saw one, you saw the other. If you looked for one, you'd find both of us. We was joined at the hip for life, and servin' double life sentences didn't change that. Anytime we get a chance, we tell young people to be careful about who they hang with. It don't matter if it's stealin', cheatin', gangs, drugs, fightin', or just hangin' out with friends and bein' somewhere you ain't got no business bein', it's easy to slip into somethin' that will mess up your life. It's even easier to slip up if you around it every day.

Jamie

We were two peas in a pod with no idea we would end up being two peas in prison. Never in a million years did we ever think our life would turn out the way it did. Some people think because of our gang activity, we were destined for prison. Being associated with a gang doesn't warrant a double life prison sentence. The whole time I was in prison, I never met anybody who was sent to prison just because they were in a gang.

Being in the streets in the projects was really no

different from being in the streets anywhere else. We've heard so many times that we're products of our environment. There were plenty other kids who grew up in the Chicago projects who never saw the inside of a jail cell, so it ain't always about the environment you're raised in. People can think whatever they want to think, but we did *not* commit armed robbery. We played the hand we were dealt and we played it the best way we knew how. There are some kids who grow up in rich and famous families that end up in drug rehab or prison, so being a product of your environment ain't always the case for how somebody's life turns out. It's easy to say, but it ain't as easy to prove. The projects don't commit crimes, the people *in* the projects do.

It was hard for Daddy to control our brothers, but he had a tight hold on us girls. Plus, we were younger. It seemed like our brothers got more freedom than we did. Daddy didn't seem to be as hard on them as he was us girls. He wanted all his kids to stay out of trouble, but he was more protective of his girls. Maybe he thought boys could protect themselves and girls *needed* to be protected. We knew we could take care of ourselves, but Daddy wasn't hearing that. We were his girls and, as far as he was concerned, it was his job to protect us and he did anything and everything to do it.

We thought about Daddy's protective ways a lot while we sat in prison, day after day, year after year. We wished Daddy would've protected us from going to prison. This goes to show that parents can protect their children as much as they can, but they can't protect them from life. Obviously, Daddy couldn't protect us from double life in prison. The life our parents gave us may not have been the life they planned, but it happened. We didn't meet anybody in prison who planned to go to prison, and we don't think any sane parent plans for their kids to go to prison. Daddy tried so hard to protect us from the outside world that he literally kept us inside. Little did he know that his efforts would land us inside a prison.

We lived around law-breaking neighbors, but Mama and Daddy did their best with what they had to give us a loving home. Both our parents were hard workers. Daddy worked as a house manager at the University of Illinois Hospital, and Mama worked as house manager on the home front. Daddy expected Mama to keep us in sight when he worked. Because Daddy was so protective and wanted to keep such a tight hold on us, that he tried to watch our every move. If he had his way, we would've gone to school every day, come straight home, and nothing else. Daddy didn't want us doing nothing. If he could make us sit at home all day behind locked doors just to keep us safe and out of trouble, he would've. We knew the streets looked for trouble whether we were looking for trouble or not, so we had to be creative in finding ways to keep ourselves busy and out of trouble.

We wanted to keep Daddy's mind at ease, so we eventually found a new interest and one that kept us off the streets like Daddy wanted. We knew Daddy wouldn't be happy with our new choice of entertainment, but it sure was entertaining for us. It was our new interest that made Daddy want to move us from Chicago to Mississippi. Boys, boys, boys! If Daddy had found out either one of us was even *thinking* about a boy, he would have shipped us off to a boarding school. Daddy tried to protect us the best way he knew how, but while Daddy was trying to protect us from the boys in the streets, he forgot to look for the boys next door. Right under Daddy's nose, we were being fast-tailed and hot.

Gladys

A real cute boy lived next door to us, and he and Jamie got to be good friends. It didn't take but a minute for Jamie to fall in love, and the boy next door all of a sudden was her "boyfriend." Daddy thought they was just friendly neighbors. They was friendly neighbors alright...too friendly. It's funny how parents don't see what's right in front of 'em. Daddy was protective of his girls, like any lovin' father would be, but while he was busy bein' protective, Jamie was gettin' busy havin' unprotected sex right next door.

Jamie

Mama noticed I hadn't asked for any sanitary pads for a couple of months, so she decided to take me to the doctor. Mama didn't waste no time getting me there and it seemed like she was in a hurry to get there. While driving to the doctor's office, we got stopped by the police for speeding and this upset Mama more than she already was. When we made it to the doctor's office, the nurse told us the doctor was out for a couple of hours and we'd have to come back. This made Mama mad, too. I kept telling Mama we didn't have to go back to the doctor's office because nothing was wrong with me. Mama paid me no mind, and we went right back to the doctor's office. Mama's anger and silence was scaring me. I already knew what Mama was trying to find out, and there was no way out of my situation.

I had to pee in a cup, and the doctor came in the room a little while later with the results. It was confirmed – I was pregnant. I thought of a quick way out of my situation and before I knew it, I told the doctor he was lying because I hadn't done nothing. I argued that doctor down until Mama slapped the mess out of me. She was already mad from the speeding ticket and the long wait, then I had the nerve to lie. I know that slap made Mama feel good because she slapped me across my face real good and hard. Mama slapped my face because she was upset, but mostly because I lied to her.

We were taught not to lie. Mama would always say there were too many kids in the house for her to keep up with a bunch of lies, so lying wasn't tolerated in our house. Daddy said lies would taint our character because nobody would ever believe anything we said. I knew I was in trouble with Mama as soon as that lie crossed my lips, but her hand across my face reminded me of Daddy's teaching to tell the truth.

For a mother to find out her thirteen-year-old daughter is pregnant must be devastating. Mama probably wanted to cuss me out, but since we were in the doctor's office she didn't. But her anger gave her hand permission to light my face up! I wanted to believe my own lie because the reality of it all was too much for my thirteen-year-old mind to take in. I got pregnant my *first* time having sex. I was thirteen and he was sixteen. Having sex at thirteen years old was the beginning of my disobedience. I paid for that one wrong decision, to have sex, for the rest of my life. I knew better, but I didn't care. I was hard-headed and didn't want to listen to my parents. I was only thirteen years old, but I thought I was grown. Actually, I *knew* I was grown. And as far as I was concerned, Mama and Daddy didn't know what they were talking about, and they never made any sense to me.

I thought my father was just being too strict, and I didn't understand why I couldn't have a boyfriend. My friends had boyfriends, so why did I have to be different? Instead of being obedient and listening to Daddy, I chose to sneak and have a boyfriend anyway. My boyfriend made me happy, so I couldn't understand why Daddy wouldn't want me to be happy. I tried to outsmart Mama and Daddy, but I was the one that got tricked.

My so-called boyfriend told me we were going to play house. That should've been a red flag right there. What sixteen-year-old *boy* wants to play house? Playing house turned into the mom and dad going to bed. That should've been red flag number two. There is no reason a teenage boy would want to be in bed with a girl except for one reason – sex. We were in bed and one thing led to another. He did what he wanted to do with my body and he told me to get out the house.

He hurt me physically and emotionally. I thought he cared about me. I thought he was supposed to be my "boyfriend." He was a boy alright, but he sure wasn't being no kind of friend. I didn't pay attention to the red flags, and I let him use my body and leave me. I'm sure he went on to the next girl who was looking for someone to make her feel special. I wished I could turn back the hands of time, but it was too late. It was no telling what Daddy was going to do when he found out I got pregnant, so me and Gladys hid under the bed together. If Daddy was going to kill one of us, he ould have to kill both of us. We held hands and cried under that bed until Daddy got home.

Gladys

I was just as scared as Jamie was. We knew Daddy was gon' go off and I wasn't 'bout to let my sister go through that by herself. When Daddy got home from work, we heard Mama talkin' to him, and Daddy was quick to blame Mama for Jamie's pregnancy. Daddy expected Mama to watch us every minute of the day since she was at home with us. Daddy expected her to keep her eyes on us while he was out workin'. Daddy did all he could to protect us from somethin' like this happenin' so when he heard the news, he didn't wanna believe it. Daddy put the blame on Mama, knowin' good and well that she ain't have nothin' to do with Jamie havin' sex and gettin'pregnant.

Jamie

Daddy didn't kill us, but the news killed him. Daddy was so heart-broken, he left the house for two days. This was the first time one of his girls really hurt him, and he had a hard time dealing with it. He felt like he failed us as a father, and we felt bad for causing him so much pain. We had never seen Daddy like that before. Daddy was mad at me my entire nine months. I couldn't believe I was the cause of Daddy's pain, and I really couldn't believe I got pregnant my first time having sex.

When it was time to deliver my baby, I was scared and Mama was, too. I heard her on the phone with Daddy saying how scared she was. I don't know what Daddy said to Mama, but it didn't help her or me. The fact that Mama was scared made me even more scared. I never felt so scared in my life! She was supposed to be helping me, but couldn't find the strength to help herself. I was too scared to feel bad for her. After all the fights Mama had with Daddy, I couldn't believe *she* was actually scared, but she was. As a mother, I guess it was okay for her to be in pain, but not her thirteen-year-old daughter. At least, not *this* kind of pain. Mama was crying and because she wasn't no help to me, I just knew I was about to die. I didn't know what to expect, what to think, or what to do. Mama wasn't no help!

Mama finally called her friend, Eula Ann, because she just couldn't handle it all by herself. It was a scary time for both of us. Mama's friend came and showed me how to breathe through each contraction. I didn't take childbirth classes, so all this breathing was new to me. I can't remember if it helped me feel any better or not, but I know having Eula Ann there with me made me and Mama feel a whole lot better. I remember a lot of pressure between my legs and it felt like I had to boo-boo real bad, so when I was told to push, I was afraid I would mess all over myself. I didn't know this was the baby coming. I couldn't understand where all the pain was coming from, but my whole body was in pain. It hurt like hell, and I was scared to death. I just wanted it to all be over and I remember wishing I had never had sex, but it was too late – way too late. After too many hours, too much pain, and a whole lot of fear, it was finally over. At thirteen years old, I gave birth to a baby girl.

Because I was so thankful for Mama's friend being there, I gave my daughter her middle name, Ann. I named my newborn baby girl, Jamicee Ann. I kept looking at her little face and couldn't believe she was mine. I had a daughter. I knew I was too young, but there she was in my arms – alive and in the flesh. I was still scared, but it was a different kind of scared. Now that my baby was here, I didn't know what to do with her. I didn't know how to take care of her, but I knew Mama would help me. I knew Mama would be more help to me than she was in the hospital.

Daddy finally came around after Jamicee Ann was born. He took one look at her and fell in love. He loved his grandbaby. You would think Jesus was born in our house by the way Daddy was acting. Mama would dress Jamicee so cute, and Daddy would come in from work every day and yell, "Hey, Daddy's Red!" He called her Red because of her light skin tone. Seeing Jamicee was the highlight of Daddy's day after a long day at work.

Mama didn't really teach me how to take care of Jamicee like I thought she would. Instead, she took care of Jamicee herself. Mama felt like I needed to still be a child since I was only thirteen. Jamicee's crib was in Mama and Daddy's room, so I didn't have to get up when she cried. Mama fed her, clothed her, and changed her. It was like Mama had the baby instead of me.

I thought all the pain I went through would keep me from having sex, but it didn't. I forgot about that pain and forgot about the consequences of having sex, so I kept having sex and had two more kids. Nothing really changed for me after having my kids because Mama and Daddy kept them for me. Mama and Daddy did everything for my kids. I was still able to go to school, be with my friends, and be a child just like Mama wanted me to be. Mama seemed to enjoy taking care of my kids, and Daddy did too. Gladys was always there for me, and we did everything together. Unfortunately, just like her big sister, Gladys found herself pregnant at thirteen years old, too. We were children having children.

Gladys

Jamie wasn't the only one bein' fast, I had my eye on a real cute fifteen-year-old boy. He was popular 'cause he played basketball and wore nice clothes. He had game, and he was a playa. His mom was a nurse, and was always workin', so he took advantage of bein' home alone, and convinced me to come over one day to play strip poker. One thing led to another.

Havin' a baby at a early age was depressin' for me 'cause I didn't know how to be a Mother. I was scared to death. I was a baby myself. When I first found out I was pregnant, I didn't tell nobody except my baby's daddy and he thought I was lyin'. I knew he was the daddy 'cause he was the first and only man I had ever been with. I was too scared to tell anybody else. I knew Daddy would kill me especially since Jamie was already havin' babies. He probably hoped I had learned from Jamie, but instead I made the same mistake. I was the baby girl, and he never expected me to be havin' sex, and he sho' didn't expect me to pop up pregnant.

I kept my secret to myself as long as I could until the school called and told Mama I kept gettin' sick. Mama made my brother, Terry, take me to the doctor. Me bein' pregnant never crossed Mama's mind, which is probably why she had my brother take me to see the doctor. Well, the doctor told me what I already knew. I was thirteen and pregnant. When me and Terry got home, all hell broke loose. Mama and Daddy had a big fight, and Daddy told Mama it was her fault – again. I felt sorry for Mama 'cause she got blamed for everything. Daddy blamed Jamie, too. He knew we did everything together, so he assumed we had planned to get pregnant together. Daddy was wrong. We didn't plan to get pregnant 'cause we didn't even think we could *get* pregnant. This kinda thing happened to other girls, not us.

Daddy was so mad, he left the house like he did for Jamie's first baby, but this time he came back with $300 for me to get rid of my baby. I cried and cried, and told Daddy I wanted my baby. Mama said she didn't believe in killin' kids and said I could keep my baby. Daddy was scared, hurt, and didn't know how to deal with both of his girls havin' babies at such a young age, but I knew I couldn't kill my baby. I didn't care how Daddy felt - abortion wasn't an option for me. I wasn't ready to take care of no baby, but I knew I wanted to keep my baby. Mama said she would raise the baby herself, and that convinced Daddy to let me keep my baby. Daddy couldn't stand the sight of his little girls havin' anything besides a doll in our hands, but we had real live dolls. Mama had her hands full, but she did what she knew to do – and that was to take care of her kids, and now her grandkids.

I went back to school, but every day when I came home, I did my best to help take care of my baby girl. She was like a baby doll to me, and it scared me that she was so real. I was so happy that I had Mama and Daddy's help 'cause I knew I couldn't do it by myself. It was real hard takin' care of a baby when I was practically a baby myself. Daddy got over his anger and loved my daughter, Olivia, like she was his own, just like he did with Jamie's first baby. Olivia's daddy wasn't ready to step up and be a father, but his mom helped out a lot. Olivia was her first grandbaby, so she did as much as she could to help out. Olivia's Daddy is still a playa, and has kids all over Chicago.

~

Our pregnancies at such an early age did something to Daddy that we never really understood. Daddy only wanted the best for us, but we thought he was going to lose his mind over us; he just wasn't the same. He felt like a failure, but seeing his grandchildren gave him a little hope for the future of his family. He knew we needed him more than ever, and now he had grandchildren who needed him, too. Daddy didn't lighten up on his protection plan for us, and when his grandchildren came, he had even more reason to protect his family.

Daddy had reached his limit with us and couldn't take it anymore. He had enough. He had also reached his limit with the Chicago life, the projects, and trying to protect his girls from the crime-filled streets. Our older siblings were off doing their own thing, and Daddy refused to lose us to the streets. He was not about to let us get killed or caught up in drugs, and now he had his grandchildren to protect. Daddy didn't want this life for his family, so he unexpectedly retired from his job at the hospital and decided to move the family to Mississippi, his home. Daddy's passion to protect his family was how we ended up in Mississippi in the first place.

Mississippi? When Daddy first told us we were moving from Chicago to Mississippi, we did *not* want to go. It was okay for us to visit, but not to live. We didn't want to leave the fast city life for the slow country living. We didn't want to leave the projects for the pastures, but we didn't have a choice. Boonanie refused to go, so she ran away from home. Her life in Chicago wasn't much of a life on drugs, but it was *her* life and she didn't want to leave it. Boonanie was eighteen, so Daddy didn't try to stop her from running away. He said, "She'll find her way when she get hungry." Boonanie got hungry about a year after we moved to Mississippi, and found her way to the country with the rest of us.

Daddy chose Forest, Mississippi in Scott County for our new home. He hoped the South would be better for his family. After we moved and got settled, we didn't know which was better: dealing with gangs and crime, or dealing with the KKK and racism. We quickly made up our minds that we didn't like Mississippi. It was so different from Chicago. It was so slow and we had a hard time even giving Mississippi a chance. As young teenagers, we wanted to have our way, and of course nothing was going our way in Mississippi, so we made things worse by finding ways to get in trouble. We wanted to get our parents' attention because it didn't seem like they were listening to us or cared about how we felt being miserable in Mississippi. We thought we were sending a message to our parents, and hoped they'd think about moving back to Chicago, but they knew exactly what we were up to. Daddy wasn't about to move back to Chicago, so we were stuck – stuck like Mississippi mud.

We didn't have the view we had from our 15th floor window. The only thing we saw was grass, trees, a few other houses, cars, and some buildings around town. So instead of looking out our window, we would sneak out of our bedroom window. We tried our best to find something, *anything*, to get into. After a few times of sneaking out, Daddy caught us and boarded our bedroom window to keep us from sneaking out again. We didn't like being locked in at all. It was like being locked in our bedroom in Chicago and not being able to go outside.

Gladys

I thought I would go crazy bein' locked up and cooped up again. I thought Daddy had lost his mind, and I felt like I was in jail. Little did I know that that boarded bedroom window wouldn't compare to the little windows in prison covered with metal bars. Bein' locked up in my bedroom was heaven compared to bein' locked up in prison for sixteen years. I look back on things like this in my life and can't help but wonder if they was signs of what was ahead for me and my sister.

We didn't give our new Mississippi school a chance either, and our grades showed it. We just didn't care. We also missed our gang family, but leavin' Chicago was the easiest way for us to break loose from the gang 'cause they wouldn't just let us walk away. But us movin' away didn't give 'em a choice. They wasn't much of a gang anyway, and the only reason we did it was to be like our brother, Terry. Followin' behind Terry wasn't a good idea 'cause we left him somewhere in the streets of Chicago, still up to no good, so at least we was safe with Mama and Daddy.

Jamie

Our move to Mississippi brought about a lot of changes, but they weren't all good changes like Daddy expected. We wondered if we would have ended up in prison if we had stayed in Chicago. Actually, it probably would have been Mama or Daddy that ended up in prison because some nights, we thought one of them would end up killing the other. When we say there was always something going on in the projects, we meant it, and sometimes that "something going on" was right in our own house. We saw a lot of street fights from our 15th floor bedroom window, but we saw a lot of fights right in our living room between our own parents. Our parents loved each other, but they had a funny way of showing it. We not only witnessed street fighting outside our home, we witnessed street fighting in our home, too.

Love Taps

Mama and Daddy fought all the time. Fighting was just a normal part of their marriage. Well, maybe not so normal for some couples, but it was normal to our parents. Fighting was a big part of their relationship; it was some more of that "stuff" in our family. We're not talking about arguing and petty disagreements, we're talking about real fights – dirty, physical fights with fists. We wished our parents *did* argue and have disagreements, but words wasn't their thing. Exchanging words wasn't strong enough for Mama and Daddy, but exchanging love taps was more their style of fighting.

Most of the time, their fights were about money. Mama wanted to control the money, but James Rasco wasn't about to let that happen. Daddy worked hard for his money and he worked hard to control it. The fact that Daddy was buying our clothes and food wasn't enough for Mama. She wanted to decide how the money was spent, who it was spent on, and she wanted to spend it when she got ready. Instead of Daddy controlling the money, Mama wanted control.

Mama always initiated the fights because Daddy was a quiet man until he got a little alcohol in him. Daddy would hug all over us when he got drunk, but Mama would jump in the mix and mess everything up. What started out for us as a fun, loving time with Daddy turned into the perfect time for Mama to stir up a fight. Daddy had a quick temper, but it took a little something extra to stir his temper to the point where he wanted to actually fight somebody.

Seagram's Gin was Daddy's choice – his something extra. He loved himself some Seagram's, but we didn't. We knew once he got a little gin in him, mixed with some of Mama's mouth, that things in the house would change. It was something about Seagram's that took Daddy to that perfect point of being pissed. Mama knew what Seagram's did to Daddy, and she always seemed to know exactly when to pick her little petty fights and stir Daddy's drunkard anger. It was like watching a sleeping volcano wake up real slow and erupt out of the blue. We knew it was coming, we just didn't know when.

Mama and Daddy's arguments about money would always blow up into full-blown fist fights – they made sure of it. It was like they made a point to have a fight at least once a month. Sometimes we wondered who the real perpetrator of the fights were – Seagram's Gin or Evelyn Rasco, our mom. Daddy didn't want us to see him beat Mama, so he would clumsily push us in a closet or in our bedroom to keep us from watching. Of course, we would crack the door and watch anyway. Something in us made us watch our parents fight; we had to. We were scared, but we still watched. We were watching with our own eyes, but still didn't want to believe what our eyes were seeing. While we watched, we cried. We couldn't believe it. Words can't explain what the fights looked like through our young eyes. Mama and Daddy fought like cats and dogs.

It didn't seem like Daddy showed any mercy when his big fists met Mama's small face. Back and forth, the punches would flow. It was like watching a boxing match when the fighters weren't matched up right. One was heavy-weight and the other was feather-weight. It didn't seem fair; it didn't seem right. As little girls, we *knew* it wasn't right. Listening to Mama's whining whimpers after taking Daddy's solid punches would hurt us more than it probably hurt her. It was heart-breaking for us to watch. It didn't look like Daddy was holding back when he would easily knock Mama down, but we prayed some mercy was balled up in Daddy's big fists. Our hearts hurt like Mama's face *looked* like it hurt. Mama *had* to be in pain, there was no way she couldn't be, but she would always get up, and get back in the fight. She got up like she wanted more. As young girls, we never understood what was going on – it was just something that happened.

Even while Mama was fighting and crying, Mama got some good punches in, too. That woman could fight! We don't know where her little 4'9" petite frame got the strength to bear Daddy's 6' powerful punches, but she did. For as long as we can remember, our parents fought. And as unnatural as it seems, it was a natural part of our family life – our family "stuff." After the fights, our parents went to bed... in the same bed. It was crazy, but as long as they were together, we were okay. Sometimes, when the fights got real bad, Daddy would leave the house and come back the next day or just go to work. If he stayed gone too long, Mama put us up to call him because she knew he couldn't resist his girls. There were also times when Mama would leave the house and stay with one of her brothers or sisters. She was from Chicago, so she always had some place to go temporarily, but she always came back home.

The morning after the fights, we couldn't wait to see Mama to make sure she was okay. She always looked so bad. Sometimes her eyes were swollen shut and sometimes she would have a busted lip. Sometimes she could hardly move. We would just helplessly stare at her. She walked real slow like she was using her last bit of energy to put one foot in front of the other. There was no doubt Mama was in pain. She even walked like she was in pain, but in the midst of all her pain, she would tell us everything was alright. We were young, but we weren't crazy. We knew everything wasn't alright, and Mama's half-shut, black eyes proved it, but she wanted us to believe that it was. We hated to see Mama all beat up, but we didn't know what to do. Our young minds couldn't even deal with the fact that our mom had been beat up by our dad.

Sometimes when our parents fought, we would be so scared we would sneak and dial 911. But when the police came, Mama and Daddy never pressed charges. Not even the police could help Mama. Sometimes, Mama would desperately call the police herself, but still refused to press charges on Daddy. We couldn't figure out why she called them if she wouldn't let them help her. We thought maybe they were, in fact, helping her by giving her a break from the blows. Maybe Mama's 911 calls were like the bells that ring in a boxing match telling the boxers to go to their own corner, get patched up, and get ready for the next round. One time, Daddy broke one of Mama's arms and she ended up in the hospital. When the police came to the hospital to question them, Mama and Daddy covered for each other and again, and chose not to press charges. None of it made any sense to us.

We were too young to understand, and we still don't understand why our parents fought each other the way they did. We finally had to accept the fact that we had a mom that liked to fight – period. Mama was a fighter, emotionally and physically. She didn't have a problem fighting back and she held her own against an out of control drunk man named Daddy. Our parents had a love/hate relationship. We hated how they fought, but this was obviously their way of showing love. There was no other explanation for it.

Our Mama, Evelyn Rasco, loved herself a good fight and for as far back as we can remember, Mama could stir a pot of nothing and make it something to fight about. Believe it or not, in spite of all the fighting, every now and then our parents actually showed a little normal affection towards each other. On special occasions like birthdays, anniversaries, and major holidays, we got to see them kiss and hug, and sometimes even hold hands. Those *special occasion* hugs and kisses let us know our parents really did love each other. All children deserve to see a little love shown between their parents, at least sometimes.

Even though Daddy was beating Mama, it was hard for us not to love him. After the fights, Daddy would always be back to his normal quiet self. The house would go back to its normal self, too. In just a few days after the fight, it seemed like nothing ever happened. We know it might seem crazy, but it was our family "stuff," and it was normal to us. We were always relieved when the fights were over, but we knew another scheduled bout was coming. As little girls, the man beating our mom was our dad and he was the one who made sure we had everything we needed; he was our provider and our protector. Did we like to see Daddy fight Mama? Of course not, but we knew he loved us and he worked hard for his family. We knew he loved Mama too, he just had a funny way of showing it. He showed love his way, and we guess it was Mama's way, too. We always hoped that the last fight would actually be the last fight we would see, but it never was.

Actually, Mama and Daddy had something else in store. They got bored with their fist fights and took their fighting to another level. The fights must've gotten old because sadly, their fists turned into guns. Our parents went from fist fights to gun fights. Yes, gun fights with *real* guns and *real* bullets. Mama and Daddy shot each other more than a couple of times. It's a wonder our parents didn't kill each other or one of us.

Jamie

I remember a time when Mama pulled a gun out on Daddy during one of their monthly fights. Daddy grabbed Gladys and held her because he just knew Mama wasn't going to shoot him with Gladys in his arms. Gladys was about seven or eight years old. Daddy obviously didn't know his wife too good because Mama aimed and pointed that gun right at Daddy's feet and shot him dead in his foot. She didn't care if he had Gladys in his arms or not. She was going to pull that trigger and shoot him regardless. There was no escaping Mama's fury. Gladys was affected the most by Mama and Daddy's fighting and she grew up to be a fighter like Mama. Gladys would throw a punch before you knew it. In prison, Gladys' reputation was to fight now and talk later. Over the years and with age, Gladys calmed down a lot. She'll actually talk to you first and fight only to defend herself, but I wouldn't try her.

Gladys

When Mama shot Daddy, I remember my ears ringin' and Daddy sayin', "Woman are you out of your goddamn mind?" He said some other words that made my ears ring more than the sound of that gun shot. That is one childhood memory I wish I could forget. I wish I could get it outta my mind forever. Me and Daddy was okay, but I'll never get over that trauma as a kid. Little did I know I had more trauma ahead of me that was a whole lot worse than that gunshot. Now, I not only hear that gunshot in my head, but I hear the ringin' of prison bars slammin' shut – two memories I can't seem to shake.

55

~

Mama showed no fear, but for two young girls watching their parents fight with guns, we were scared out of our minds. Our family life took the meaning of dysfunction to a whole 'nother level, but we owned it. It was functional to us – more of our "stuff." The fights between our parents disturbed us, but we learned to stomach each fight. It wasn't easy, but we survived and so did Mama.

As soon as our brothers got old enough, they left the house because they didn't like how Daddy jumped on Mama. They wanted to jump on Daddy and protect Mama, but we all knew things would have gotten a whole lot worse. Our brothers respected Daddy as their step-father, but the respect stopped there. There was always a lot of tension between them, and they never had a strong father-son relationship. Regardless of the fights between Mama and Daddy, we had a good relationship with our father, but it was our relationship with Mama that we had to work on. It took us going to prison for Mama to open up and freely love us, but we don't blame her for that. We blame Aunt Gladys.

Mama did all the things a mother was supposed to do, but something was missing. We didn't feel that motherly affection from Mama. We didn't feel that motherly love and we didn't have the kind of relationship where we could go to Mama and talk to her about anything. She took real good care of us, but when it came to that mother and child bond, we didn't have it. We missed out on that bond and it took us going to prison for Mama to even tell us she loved us.

We don't blame Mama because she simply raised us like her mama raised her, and Mama had a mean mama. Mama's mama was *real* mean and hateful. She was nothing like a grandmother to us, so we called her Aunt Gladys. Yes, we called our grandmother Aunt Gladys. She was one mean, hateful woman. We remember her always showing favorites with the grandkids and we weren't on her list of favorites. Some grandkids could go in her house and get candy and some couldn't. We couldn't. Even as children, we knew her actions were wrong, and those hurtful memories are still with us. Whenever Aunt Gladys and Mama had a disagreement about something, we heard Aunt Gladys say, "Take these little bastards and go to your own house!" Aunt Gladys always talked down to Mama, and even to some of her grandkids. We hated to hear Aunt Gladys talk to Mama like that. The woman she was cussin' was her daughter, but it was our Mama, too, and we didn't like it one bit. The only time Aunt Gladys was nice to us was when we were with Daddy. Everybody respected Daddy, and was just about scared of him. Daddy didn't take no mess from nobody, not even Aunt Gladys. When Daddy talked, people listened. When he came around, you better had straightened up.

Gladys

I was named after Aunt Gladys and I hate it. I used to hate when somebody called me "Little Gladys." I never liked it 'cause she didn't show us love like Daddy's mom did, and I didn't want people to think I was like her. I ain't nothin' like Aunt Gladys. She was so mean and she treated us like we was outsiders. I never liked goin' to her house either, but sometimes Mama and Daddy made us go. The only time I didn't have a problem goin' to her house was when she cooked. I remember Aunt Gladys cookin' coon with sweet potatoes and it was so good. Man, that coon was good! She cooked a pecan pie out of this world, too, and I ain't never tasted another one like it.

~

Aunt Gladys was a little nicer to us after we got sent to prison. We found out that our mean grandmother actually had a heart capable of showing some love. Aunt Gladys let us call her from prison once a month, and she would accept the charges. We always ended the phone calls by telling her we loved her, and Aunt Gladys would come back and say, "Same too." We believe Aunt Gladys' generational curse of being so mean was passed on to Mama. Mama didn't know how to show us motherly love because she didn't get it herself. Mama did the best she could with the training she had. We never doubted Mama's love for us. We knew she had her own way of showing her children love, and so did Mama.

Mama did a good job taking care of six children, and she was always busy doing something around the house. Mama stayed busy and she was a neat freak. Mama would get on her hands and knees and clean and wax the floors until they were spotless. Those floors were so clean we could eat off of them. She was *always* picking up behind everybody and kept a clean, neat house. Everybody in the projects had roaches except us; Mama wasn't having that. Mama cleaned all the time and made sure all us kids were neat and clean, too. All six of us were always bathed, fed, and dressed nicely. It was a lot of work keeping three girls' hair looking good, but Mama made sure our hair was always combed. You would never see our hair messed up or standing on top of our head; Mama had us looking good. Mama didn't believe in leftovers either. We had a hot, home-cooked meal every day we came home from school.

MISSISSIPPI MAYHEM

We weren't the only inmates sitting in prison with unbelievable stories of our upbringing and how we ended up behind bars. We heard so many in the sixteen years we were there. A lot of inmates talked about their parents or grandparents and the lack of discipline or structure they had in their life. Everybody had a story. Although our upbringing wasn't the best, we know we were loved. Our parents didn't have the best role models or examples in their lives to pass on to us, but we're thankful for two people who we respected and loved.

With all the fighting, shooting, and "stuff" in our home, we had two very special people in our lives who gave us some stability – our grandparents on Daddy's side, Bigmama and Bigdaddy. They showed us what family life was like without all the fighting and drama. Bigmama and Bigdaddy kept us grounded, and they were the reason we didn't mind *visiting* Mississippi. We would visit once a year, in the summertime, and we looked forward to it every year. It was also a memory that got us through our long prison sentence.

Our summer trips to Mississippi took us away from the Chicago crime we were surrounded by. Mississippi was a big difference from Chicago. It was slow as corn syrup, and we missed the fast pace of Chicago, but because Bigmama and Bigdaddy were there, we learned to love it – once a year in the summertime. Unlike Chicago, we didn't see much happen in

Mississippi, and it seemed like people would sit on the porch and watch grass grow. Even from our 15th floor window we knew we would always see some kind of action going on, but not in Mississippi. The love of Bigmama and Bigdaddy made up for the lack of action. Our grandparents made us feel special, and that meant the world to us.

Bigdaddy was always busy with his farm and when he came in he relaxed. He was a loving, hard-working man, but everybody knew Bigmama ran the house. Bigmama was a praying woman. She wasn't anything like Aunt Gladys. She talked to us about Jesus and she was our example of a God-fearing woman. Bigmama would sit on her front porch, shell peas, and tell us story after story of how good God was to her. Everything we know about faith was planted by our Bigmama.

Those times in prison when we felt like giving up is when Bigmama's voice would visit us. Our faith weakened a little bit every day in prison, but we used every ounce of what she poured into us to get through those rough days and nights in prison. Bigmama taught us to seek the Light to get through dark hours – there was plenty of dark hours in prison. Bigmama's porch stories became our prison stories. We shared Bigmama's God with other inmates, and her faith flowed through the prison. We shared her stories of wisdom and faith every chance we got, and each time we shared it, we were helping ourselves to stay strong.

Bigmama is gone now and we miss her so much. She was a good woman. She gave us that motherly love and nurturing that Mama couldn't give us. Bigmama died before the family nightmare started, and we are so grateful that she died remembering our summer visits and not her visits to see us in prison. Bigmama passed away before we were convicted, sentenced, and named the "Scott Sisters."

We loved visiting Mississippi, but we had no desire to move to Mississippi. Being teenagers, we had no choice. Daddy said we were moving, so we moved. Daddy expected things to change with the move and hoped the slower pace of the small, Southern town, his home, would be best for us. Well, some things did change, but one thing didn't change – the drugs. Even in small-town Forest, Mississippi, if you wanted drugs, you could get them. The drugs followed us from the city to the country, and Gladys was the third of the siblings to be touched by drugs.

Gladys

Men was always my downfall; they was my weakness. Dealin' with no good men led me to drug dealin'. I ain't blamin' my drug use on men, but love lured me to drugs. One guy in particular introduced me to drugs. He was an older guy, and Jamie didn't like him at all 'cause she knew what his game was. This man had street smarts *and* book sense – and he used both to charm me. He got my attention with his fancy words and wisdom. He taught me a lot of things, but one thing I wished he hadn't taught me was how to get high. He taught me how to lace weed (putting crack on top of weed.) I dabbled with drugs for fun and my dabblin' turned into a depressin' dependence. I just wanted to sell drugs for the money, but I turned from bein' a seller to bein' a user. It happened so quick, and in such a strange way, that I don't even know when it happened.

I really didn't know what I was doin', but the guy that got me hooked on drugs knew exactly what was goin' on from the jump. He was a snake in the grass, and took advantage of my ignorance. Drugs ain't nothin' to play with, and it's not somethin' to try just once. My "once" turned into a once again...and again...and again. The drugs was way more powerful than my will. The drugs started makin' decisions for me; they overpowered my mind. They took control of my mind and my body. I was being controlled by somethin' I *thought* I had control of. Crack and Cocaine became my best friends, but it didn't take long to find out my friends wasn't really friends at all. My so-called friends caused me to lose everything I had.

My life was turned upside down and emptied out. I had to take care of my daughter, Olivia, so I did whatever I had to do to take care of her. but at the same time, I made sure I took care of my desperate need for drugs. When I say I did whatever I had to do, I did *whatever* was necessary, includin' sellin' my body to support my drug habit. Mama saw the life I was livin' and started takin' care of Olivia again. She didn't want Olivia being 'round the drugs and men. I loved my child, but the drugs blinded me from how I was hurtin' her. I was doing the best I could, but my best wasn't good enough. My best was my best on drugs.

I made sure Olivia was always dressed nice and fed. I made sure her physical needs was met, but I wasn't bein' the mother she needed. By lookin' at me you woulda never known I was on drugs. I was a closet addict. My parents knew what was goin' on, so they made me move out of their house. I knew havin' my own place was an invitation to get wild, so I gladly accepted the invitation. I moved out of my parents' house, without Olivia, and got buck wild. I was out of control. Daddy would say, "Gladys, you got to learn the hard way. You gon' have to hit rock bottom." I wasn't tryin' to hear Daddy. The only thing I heard was them drugs callin' my name, and I answered every call.

After a while, I hooked up with another guy and he taught me the game of drug dealin'. He was a lot older than me and ran his game on me. He taught me real good and I learned real fast. Things got worse for me. I was out there. I was livin' a deadly life that I had no idea I was livin'. I had my share of clubs, drugs, and men. Some days I didn't know if I would make it home 'cause I was with men I didn't even know. I was livin' a fast life and was always movin' 'round and gettin' deeper and deeper in drugs.

Some days I didn't know who I was with or where I was, but way in the back of my mind, I knew God had somethin' else for my life. It sounds strange, but I knew the life I was livin' wasn't my life. I refused to believe the life I felt trapped in was mine. I wanted to escape, but didn't know how. I wanted to find my way out, but I couldn't see nothin' but my next high. I knew my life had to change because of my prayin' grandmother. Bigmama's prayers had to take care of me. Her prayers *had* to somehow find me and cover me because I couldn't find myself. I wished my Daddy could have helped me, but I knew I needed to help myself. Daddy didn't recognize his own addiction, and he sho' didn't have time to notice mine.

Jamie

I never had a desire to smoke, drink, or do drugs. Mama used to cough real bad all the time, so I told myself I was never going to smoke cigarettes. I also saw what drinking did to Daddy, so I made up my mind, at an early age, that I would never drink. I saw what drugs did to my siblings, so that was enough to convince me to never try drugs. With all the drug use in our family, you would think Daddy would slow down with Sugar Hill. But instead, he continued to feed his own addiction of making money, and he was bigger than big in Forest.

~

Mama was known as the "First Lady" of Sugar Hill, but she started to fear for Daddy's life and the safety of the family. She started to see what all the money was doing to the family. It was good for a while, but it started taking a toll on the well-being of all of us. Mama cooked at Sugar Hill and mainly watched Daddy's back, but when she realized things were taking a turn, spending Sugar Hill's profits was no longer fun for her.

Daddy was in over his head and Mama was scared and threatened to leave him. Mama would accuse Daddy of trying to talk to women. She didn't want anybody else to get that money, but she was real jealous, too. She tried to watch everything Daddy did, but Daddy was the kind of man who didn't meet a stranger. He knew everybody and he talked to everybody. He made sure his customers felt comfortable. He knew if they felt at home at Sugar Hill, they'd always come back. Daddy paid no attention to Mama's bold threats to leave him. He didn't stop making money and Mama didn't leave. We never saw any signs of Daddy cheatin'. He was too busy making money. If Daddy was having an affair, it was with the dollar bill. He respected his family more than anything and never did anything to embarrass Mama or the family name.

Mama stood by her man in fear of his safety. She knew Daddy was in too deep to turn around. Daddy was addicted to making money. His love for the dollar bill was controlling his every move. Everything he did was about making a dollar. We wished Daddy had other ways to make money, but it was too late. He needed a stronger intervention than his family begging him to slow down.

Daddy kept all his money buried in the woods for a long time. For as long as we remember, Daddy didn't use a bank. His outdoors savings account started after one of his fights with Mama. Mama was mad, and took all the money out the bank. When Daddy found out, he never deposited another penny. Whenever we needed money, he would go outside and come back in a short time. We knew he went to his deposit spot in the woods. Daddy kept thousands and thousands of dollars in the woods, and never worried about anybody finding it. If anybody knew about Daddy's outside bank, they were too scared to touch it. Nobody messed with Daddy, and his Sugar Hill regulars had his back – as much as they could.

One evening, a well-known drug dealer was shot and killed in Sugar Hill. We always had a feeling that someone would get hurt, but we never thought anyone would get killed. This killing gave the Scott County Sheriff's Department a reason to put a pad lock on the front door of Sugar Hill. The jealous town officials finally got what they wanted, which was to put an end to Daddy's cash flow. Since they weren't gettin' a cut, they wanted the place shut down. Forest Mississippi's hot spot, Sugar Hill, was closed down again. We were strangely relieved and thought Daddy would finally have to slow down a little. Daddy didn't see this as an end to making money, but the beginning of something new. Instead of the night life, Daddy began another life – selling drugs.

Daddy had always been against selling drugs, even though he knew it was happening on Sugar Hill property. He never participated in drug use because he saw what it did to his family; however his addiction to making money opened the doors to his next money-making scheme. A lot of Daddy's Chicago drug-dealing friends told him how much money he could make selling drugs. They knew Daddy was all about making a dollar and they knew he was good at it. Even Gladys expressed to Daddy how easy selling drugs and making money was for her. With a little coaching from his baby girl, Gladys, and his high roller friends, Daddy became one of the biggest drug lords in the area. Before long, Daddy was transporting drugs across several counties.

We don't know where Daddy got the idea, but he hid the drugs in the tires of eighteen-wheeler trucks. Daddy had a full-blown drug business and never got caught. Well, there was one time Daddy got caught with drugs. The FBI and Sheriff's Department raided Daddy's house and found drugs in a pill bottle in the freezer part of the refrigerator. Daddy didn't go to jail. He did what he always did to get out of trouble. Daddy knew who to talk to and how. Of course, having money always helped him out of everything. Money talks.

With all the drugs around us, we should've seen the drug business coming during the Sugar Hill days, but we didn't. Well, maybe we did and didn't want to accept it or just refused to believe it. Addicts will do almost anything to feed their pleasure, and Daddy's pleasure was making money. We were young and all we knew was that our Daddy was "the man" in Forest, Mississippi. We had everything we wanted plus some. Money wasn't an issue for our family and we never worried about running out. This is why it's strange that we would get accused of robbing someone for eleven dollars. It makes no sense at all.

Again, Daddy found an avenue for cash flow and was rolling in the dough. We were proud of Daddy, but while we were strutting around like proud peacocks, his love for money was slowly destroying our family. Daddy may have been illiterate, but in our eyes, he was a smart man and we respected him. Daddy could barely sign his name, but when it came to taking care of his family, he took care of his business – his drug business. In Daddy's mind, taking care of his family was his main business. We were his priority. As long as we had everything we needed, Daddy was okay.

We were getting older, so Daddy bought two trailers and put them on his property for us to live in. Daddy was still trying to protect us. He wanted us to have our own place, but it would be on his property. No matter how old we got, Daddy always wanted to keep an eye on his girls. Daddy did his best to keep us happy, and we were. We may have been a little too happy because living alone gave us more freedom. More freedom brought more babies, and more babies brought a need for more money. A need for more money only fed Daddy's addiction.

Daddy's new source of income was another way to provide for his family. His drug sales reached across the southern states and the word got out. The word spread just like it did for Sugar Hill. Daddy had a knack for making his business successful, and again, some people weren't happy for Daddy's success.

A few Scott County officials heard about Daddy, but instead of questioning Daddy or arresting him for the massive amount of money and drugs they found in his possession, they asked for a cut of his profits. Again, Daddy flat out refused. Asking Daddy to share his money was like asking a crack head for his last rock, or like asking Daddy for one of his daughters. Daddy wasn't giving up one dollar, and because he wouldn't cooperate with these few "officials," our family become the target of daily harassment. We weren't harassed by the entire community, but by a very small group of county officials who 'ran things' in the community.

Jamie

The harassment caused Daddy to watch his family more and he finally started to see what his love of money hadn't allowed him to see earlier. He noticed how Gladys, then seventeen years old, had been slowly drawn into a deep hole of drug addiction that she couldn't climb out of.

Daddy quickly checked Gladys in a rehabilitation center, in Crystal Springs, Mississippi, hoping she would be okay. He knew he couldn't help her, and he probably felt responsible since he was so busy with Sugar Hill, he didn't see what was going on with us. I was surprised he didn't blame Mama like he blamed her for everything else. Gladys didn't want to go, but didn't have a choice. Daddy made her go, and didn't care how much she fought him about it. Gladys wasn't in the rehab center long before she started calling Daddy whining and complaining about coming home. Gladys found herself locked up again.

Gladys

Even though Daddy checked me in rehab, I knew he would come and get me if I told him I was bein' mistreated in the center. If me or Jamie called for Daddy's help, he always came to our rescue. I knew I needed help gettin' off drugs, but I couldn't stand not bein' able to go nowhere or do nothin'. I felt like I was in jail or somethin'. It was a horrible feelin'.

I called Daddy and told him the staff was tryin' to kill me. I even told him they were burnin' crosses in the front yard of the rehab center. I lied to Daddy and made up stories I knew he probably wouldn't believe, but I was desperate to get out. I couldn't handle bein' locked up. I tugged at Daddy's heart long enough to convince him to come pick me up. He told me he was comin' for me, but I didn't believe him because I knew he wanted me to get better. I packed my stuff and walked right out the front door of the rehab center, and I kept walkin'. I had to get the hell out of there, and when Daddy got there, he was shocked to find out I had already left.

Jamie

I went with Daddy to pick Gladys up from the rehab center. We didn't know what to think when we heard Gladys had left. Where was my sister? We knew she had a friend in Crystal Springs, so if we found Gladys' friend, we would find Gladys because she didn't know nobody else in that city. After some searching and calling round, we found Gladys' friend and, just as we thought, we found Gladys, too. I was so happy to see that she was okay. Gladys was surprised and happy to see us. Daddy didn't take Gladys back to the center like I thought he should've. Daddy was always rescuing us. Gladys went home with us, and never did drugs again. It was hard to believe, but we didn't question how she did it. We were just happy Gladys was back to being Gladys. The threat of being locked up in a rehab center was obviously rehab enough for Gladys. Being locked up probably scared her straight, and even though Daddy thought he was protecting Gladys by bringing her home, Gladys needed protection from the drugs. Gladys needed protection from herself.

~

We have reason to believe that Daddy's lifestyle choices and his love for making money paved a clear pathway for us to prison. Yes, we made some bad choices, but we did *not* commit armed robbery. The reputation of our family has followed us and blemished our character; it stained us and made us a target. It was easy to place accusations on Jamie and Gladys Scott because of who we were in the community, or should we say who our *father* was. "Be careful of the company you keep," "Guilty by association," "Birds of a feather flock together," "If it looks like a duck and quacks like a duck, then it's a duck!" These are clichés, but each one of them has its own truth.

We loved and respected our father, yet as we grew older and became more aware of our surroundings, our relationship with the man we grew up loving and respecting turned into a love-hate relationship. Daddy always provided for our family, but his choice of provision caused our family a lifetime of pain and a double life prison sentence for us. We saw the things our father got away with because of his money. We saw the dirty law at work. We experienced the dirty system and the injustice in the court system. Daddy was

72

caught in several drug raids, but the cases were always dropped because of the crooked lawyers Daddy hired to represent him. Knowing the right people and having the right amount of money that talked kept Daddy out of jail.

We wondered if we paid for the crimes daddy didn't. We also wondered if money could have kept us out of prison. We wondered things about Daddy that made us feel guilty for thinking them. But sitting in prison year after year, for no reason at all, we couldn't help but wonder about our father's role in our prison sentence. We were his "girls," but we ended up being his "girls" sitting in prison. Daddy didn't rescue us because he had something else on his mind. That "something" must've been serious because it occupied his mind heavily, and took his attention away from us. We noticed that "something" during our trial.

The Trial

Five months passed after we were indicted. Our trial began on October 4, 1994. We were anxious for it to be over. The whole court process was strange to us, almost foreign. After several jurors were passed over and others were accepted, the State and Defense Attorney finally agreed on twelve jurors for our case. Mississippi law permits juries to recommend a life-sentence for armed robbery, so we hoped and prayed for jurors that would hear only the truth in our case. The facts would surely show our innocence. Five black jurors and seven white jurors held our life in their hands.

Circuit Judge Marcus Gordon presided over our case, and he had a history of racially biased rulings including a KKK murderer of three civil rights workers that he gave bail to.

It wasn't the judge we had to worry about, but because of the Mississippi law, the jury would decide our future. They would decide whether we had life in prison or not. We always hear that the race card was played in our case. Was it? The sheriff that knocked on our door that Christmas Eve in 1993 was a black man. He was also one of the sheriffs who initially questioned us at the station. The two men who actually committed the crime and lied on us were black. Would the case have gone differently if we were another race? We believe so, however, race wasn't the only card played in this blatant case of injustice. Justice itself showed its true color – a repulsive, intimidating, and hostile color – you pick the shade.

"There is no greater form of violence than injustice."

NAACP www.naacp.org

The proceedings began. We sat in court not really understanding what was going on, but listening as carefully as we could. The few short days we spent in that court room seemed longer than the fourteen days we spent in the county jail. We watched and listened, but still didn't fully comprehend what was going on. All we knew is that we were innocent – nothing else mattered to us. We couldn't believe we were involved in an actual court case. This wasn't a Perry Mason television show, it was our life. It was real, but at the same time it felt unreal. Daddy was in court with us, but he didn't let Mama come to the courthouse because he was afraid she would get loud and go off on somebody. Mama didn't hold her tongue for nobody and we both knew she could stir up some mess in a minute, especially when it came to her children, so we were okay with her not sitting in court with us. We knew we had her support whether she was in court with us or not.

Daddy and his sister, Louella, sat in court with us. We hoped they understood what was going on better than we did. We occasionally looked back at them hoping to see some signs of hope on their faces. We didn't see a glimpse of hope, but we saw a lot of fear, which confused us and made us more afraid than we already were. But deep down inside, we both knew Daddy would somehow rescue us. All of our hope was in him since he had never let us down before. Whenever Daddy had to deal with the law, he always appeared so strong and confident, but this time was different. Daddy showed us no signs of comfort. The man that had always been there for us couldn't give us a signal or a hint that everything would be okay, yet we still trusted him and believed in him.

Daddy always handled his business. Daddy *never* showed fear...he always put fear in everybody else. People were even afraid to approach Daddy on his land because they knew he would protect his family and possessions at all costs. If you weren't invited to Daddy's house, you had better not show up unannounced because he would meet you with his gun and threaten to shoot. This fear on Daddy's face was new to us. We never saw that side of him, and we kept waiting for the man we grew up with to show up. For the first time, it seemed like his hands were tied by the ropes of a justice he had never met before. Daddy's connections were obviously disconnected, and it seemed like the future of our lives rested with twelve strangers called the jury.

The two young men, co-defendants, who supposedly committed the armed robbery with us were in court, but only one was questioned during the trial. These were the only two witnesses the State had. The co-defendant that spoke in court was completely dishonest and gave conflicting testimonies. We sat in shock, unable to say a word, as we listened to the lies. We were informed that he had written a statement the night of the crime, but later found out his testimony in court didn't come close to the statement he wrote. Although he was under oath, important facts he mentioned on the stand were *not* mentioned in his original statement to the sheriffs. He was playing with our life, and we prayed no one would believe his testimony, which was packed full of holes. The DA tried his best to make us seem as guilty as possible through his questioning of the co-defendant, but when the co-defendant was cross examined by our attorney, his story completely crumbled. It was obvious that the co-defendant was coerced – even threatened to make damaging statements against us. It was hard to sit and not say a word. We both wanted to yell out from across the courtroom "Stop lying!"

Jamie

I could tell Gladys was ready to fight, but we had to sit and be quiet. I wondered why the co-defendant wasn't telling the truth. Me and Gladys just continued to sit in total disbelief as we listened to the false accusations – the lies. I couldn't believe it. Dear God, why is this happening?

~

As the case continued, it was revealed that the co-defendants, ages eighteen and fourteen, admitted to entering a plea of guilty to the charges in exchange for a sentence of only eight years in prison. In order to receive the lesser sentence, they first had to testify against us. Something just didn't seem right. They get an eight year sentence and we get double life? Unbelievable. We didn't know much about the justice system, but we were finding out first-hand that the justice system wasn't fair.

One of the co-defendants shamefully confessed to signing another statement he didn't even read. He admitted being told if he signed the statement, which he agreed wasn't even his handwriting, he would be released from prison the next day. Who wouldn't sign a document in exchange for their freedom? Although he agreed and signed the statement, the promise of being released was not kept; he remained in prison. The fourteen-year-old boy also testified that if he didn't agree to cooperate, he was told he'd be sent to Parchman Prison and made into a female.

Parchman is the oldest and the only maximum prison for men in the state of Mississippi. In other words, he was threatened to be sexually abused and raped repeatedly if he didn't help the State find us guilty of the crime he had already admitted to committing. We couldn't believe this when we first heard it. Why did it seem so important that we be sent to prison? Dear God, why? And why wasn't Daddy going off like a mad man like he always did when somebody was doing something wrong against his family? Nobody messed with Daddy's family, but it was obvious that something or somebody was messing with Daddy's head.

In the co-defendants' actual statement made the night of the crime, there was no mention of either of us being involved in the robbery. Our names were not mentioned at all. The co-defendant confessed to the armed robbery. However in court, the statement he signed without reading was presented instead – not his own statement. The co-defendant even admitted, while under oath, that the statement he signed without reading was *not* in his handwriting. He stated he only signed the false statement because he was promised he would receive the minimum of eight years for the crime *he* committed. He was afraid. No, he was terrified for his life behind bars. What fourteen-year-old wouldn't be?

The false statement that was presented in court showed us guilty of the crime. Where is the justice? Was this a set-up, a pay-back, deliberate injustice, or a combination of the three? Did anyone in the court hear what the fourteen-year-old said? Was the jury paying close attention? Was the jury paying attention at all? Did they care about the facts? The co-defendants obviously didn't give a damn about us, but we were hoping the jury would. We had no choice but to believe the jury would do their job and hear the facts.

We didn't testify in court. We were advised by our attorneys not to. We didn't even ask why because we thought they had our back. No, we *knew* our attorneys had our back. Our innocence fed our confidence, and gave us the strength to sit in court and listen to all the lies being told. Our innocence gave us courage to not worry about being sent to prison. Our innocence convinced us that Daddy was okay because he believed in our innocence, too. If Daddy could sit in court and not say a word, we could too.

This book is our opportunity to take the stand, without interruption and without someone attempting to twist our words or twist the truth. What really happened the night of the armed robbery? This is the truth, the whole truth, and nothing but the truth, so help us God.

Jamie

The evening of the night in question, the gas in my trailer heating system ran out. It was a very cold, December night and it was supposed to be getting colder, so the priority that night was finding propane so me and my kids wouldn't be cold. Daddy recommended the "gas man" to get propane from. Gladys and I took our kids next door to our parents, and we were on our way. Gladys went with me because that's just the way we were. We did everything together – everything.

Gladys

The place where the "gas man" sold propane was already closed for the night, but he was known to fill tanks up from his home, on the side, so we drove to his house. He wasn't home, so we left the "gas man's" house and started back home since we didn't know no other place to get gas. We decided to stop by the mini mart for nothin' in particular, just somethin' to snack on while drivin' back home. We made our purchase in the store, walked out of the store back to Jamie's car to leave, but Jamie's car wouldn't start.

Jamie

We tried a couple of times to start the car, but it wouldn't turn over. Gladys saw two guys she used to work with and offered them ten dollars to give us a ride home. We wanted to pay the guys because Daddy taught us to never look for a handout. We paid for everything we needed. The two men agreed to give us a ride, but getting us back home wasn't their main concern. Having a good time and taking a joy ride was. The driver wanted to relax and drink beer, so Gladys offered to drive. Gladys loved to drive and would drive anybody's car that let her. I got in the back seat and we were both happy to be on our way back home, but that wasn't the case.

It wasn't long before I was fighting off the guy in the back seat with me. I had to keep pushing and prying him off of me. I wasn't in the mood for nonsense. All I wanted was some gas for heat in my house and a ride home, but the guy had a one-track mind and wasn't hearing my rejections. He just kept trying to get with me. He kept touching me inappropriately and even offered me money to have sex with him. Gladys was just busy driving and talking and didn't notice what was going on with me in the back seat. I was getting pissed off, so I faked being sick so he would leave me alone. I told Gladys I needed to throw up, so she would stop the car. When the car stopped, I jumped out and Gladys followed me. We weren't too far from home, so we started walking and talking about what was going on with me in the back seat.

~

While we walked away, the two men began yelling offensive words at us and calling us names. We assumed they were mad because we didn't let them have their way with us. They were looking for a good time with easy women and we were looking for a ride home back to our kids. It was cold, but we started our walk back home. We looked back and noticed another car approaching the car we jumped out of, but we just kept walking. We weren't about to stop. We had about a half a mile to walk, but we finally made it home safe and sound – without gas and without the car. Daddy plugged up portable heaters, and said he would get the gas and the car the next day. That's it. That is what happened the night of the crime, and we were completely unaware of any armed robbery that happened that night.

The truth shall set you free. Well, it should, but it didn't. Not for us. The jury returned to the courtroom after deliberating for a quick thirty minutes. We didn't know if the

81

short deliberation was a good thing or not. All we knew is that the jury made a decision about the future of our life in half an hour, so they must have known, without a doubt, that we were innocent. Anyone sitting in that courtroom, that listened to the facts, would know we were innocent. We held our breath and prayed as the jury walked in, one by one. We tried to read their faces, but they showed no sign of their decision or our future. We looked back at Daddy and he showed no sign of life – he sat like a zombie. Daddy wasn't giving us any sign of assurance that everything was going to be okay. His head was still down. Daddy wasn't Daddy.

The moment came for the reading of the verdict, and our hearts seemed to be beating in unison – fast and hard. We didn't look at each other or speak, but we both knew what the other was thinking: We can finally get on with our lives and put all this confusion and mess behind us. We anxiously listened, and we heard the one word that sent us to prison... GUILTY. The jury found us guilty. In spite of the testimonies, lies, and false statements from the witnesses, the jury found us guilty and we were each sentenced to *double* life in prison. Not life in prison, but double life. The jury chose to ignore the truth. At that moment, we were convinced that it's true that justice is blind – blind to the truth. GUILTY. *Jesus help us!*

Gladys

I was in shock – complete shock. My heart felt like it was down in my stomach. I was so hurt and couldn't believe the jury found us guilty. I couldn't believe it. I ain't never had a loss for words, but I remember bein' shocked and speechless. I couldn't think straight. I couldn't believe what I heard.

Jamie

I couldn't breathe. There was an indescribable feeling in my throat. I felt like I was being choked. I never had an out-of-body experience, but I felt like I was having one. I couldn't feel my body at all. I was wondering how and why this was happening to me. I couldn't even talk; nothing would come out of my mouth. Words can't explain how I felt at that moment.

~

GUILTY. After hearing the guilty verdict, we looked back at Daddy and he still hadn't changed his posture. It was like he had died with his head down. Daddy never made eye contact with us. Daddy had always come to our rescue, but this time it seemed like he couldn't rescue himself from whatever it was that had a hold on him. What was it? Shame? Frustration? Helplessness? We didn't understand what was going on with Daddy, but at that time, we realized we needed to focus more on what was going on with us. We had spent so much time trying to process what was going on with Daddy that now it was time to try to process what was going on with us. Our aunt sat next to Daddy with tears in her eyes and she looked stunned. We were just as stunned. We couldn't believe it. We were speechless and in complete disbelief. The officers didn't waste any time escorting us out of the courtroom. They didn't even give us time to say goodbye. Both of us literally passed out. *Jesus, help us!*

We were snatched away from our parents, our children, our life. *Dear God, what is going on?* We kept hearing the "GUILTY" verdict over and over in our heads. It just didn't seem real. We refused to believe it was happening, but we couldn't ignore the reality of it all. We were going to prison for life – double life. We didn't talk to each other, but again, we knew what the other was thinking.

Feeling numb and empty inside, we felt hate for all law enforcement. We knew something could've been done to keep us out of prison. We knew it. We saw Daddy avoid jail time too many times. We saw him talk his way out of possession of drugs, selling alcohol, and probably some other things we probably didn't know nothing about. We knew we didn't have to go to prison, but we were on our way. Fast talking and the dirty law didn't help us escape from our double life prison sentence. We continued to question God. *Dear God, what in hell is going on?* Will somebody please wake us up from this nightmare! Will somebody please tell the jury we're innocent?

An application for clemency was soon filed – it, too, was ignored just at the jury ignored the truth in court. Numerous letters were written and submitted on our behalf, only to be ignored with all the other proof of innocence that was submitted.

The actual case transcripts and a signed affidavit are

available for public viewing on the Internet; however, we

have

made excerpts from the transcript and a copy of the affidavit

available in the index.

How in the world do we say goodbye for life? How do we prepare to walk away from our life? How do we walk away from our young kids? How do we serve a life sentence? How do we serve *two* life sentences? How long is *double* life? How many days is that? How many years? How do we count double life? Do we take a leave of absence from our jobs? Will we be forgotten? At ages nineteen and twenty-one, we should've been preparing for our future and we were – our future in prison. We had to prepare to say goodbye – for life. How do we hug our kids for the last time? How do we apologize for something we *didn't* do? Who do we talk to for another chance to prove our innocence? Why didn't we tell our side of the story in court? Who will listen? Where is God?

We were taken to the county jail first and had to spend about two or three weeks there before they transported us to prison. We found ourselves in the same jail we were in on Christmas Eve – the jail we said we never wanted to see again and would never go back to. We raised hell and caused chaos the whole time we were there. We were mad at the world and we wanted to let the world know. We couldn't believe this was happening to us and we weren't going to stand by and just let it happen. Making noise was the only thing we could do to try to get some attention, but nobody paid us any.

85

Nobody cared that we were innocent. Nobody believed we were innocent. We were going to prison for armed robbery... for *only* eleven dollars.

The whole time we were in the county jail, Daddy didn't come to see us. He couldn't handle it. Daddy knew if he came around, the sheriffs would provoke him to say or do something he would regret. Daddy didn't want to make matters worse for us or get himself in trouble. The sheriff's department always messed with Daddy and since Daddy had a temper, it was best for him to stay away. Daddy couldn't stand to see us in jail, so it was just easier for him to not come around.

Jamie

I was ready to leave Scott County. They burned me and did me wrong, I wanted to be anywhere besides that small, Redneck town.

Gladys

Sittin' in jail for the second time, everything started to hit me. I realized I wasn't goin' back home. I *really* wasn't goin' home. Since I was pregnant, the sheriffs didn't want to be responsible for anythin' that happened to me, so they had planned to transport us to prison as soon as they could. We were makin' so much noise that they was ready for us to go.

~

We would be going to the Central Mississippi Correctional Facility (CMCF) in Pearl, Mississippi (Rankin County). CMCF is the only facility for female prisoners in Mississippi. It's also a facility for minimum-, medium-, and some maximum-security male criminals. If that's not enough criminals for you, CMCF is also the state of Mississippi's Death Row prison. We were nineteen and twenty-one and we were going to prison. We were going to prison with actual criminals – with criminals on Death Row. We were going to prison – for life. *Why us, Lord?* Out of all the people in the world, why were we convicted of a crime we didn't commit and sentenced to double life in prison. *Dear God, why us?*

The day before we transferred from the county jail to prison, we were told that Rankin County would be waiting on us and we were given a list of things we could take with us like cigarettes, personal items, and $20. The sheriffs told us to call our family to let them know we would be leaving the next morning.

Gladys

I called Mama and told her we was gettin' ready to go, and she cried. She was so mad with Daddy for what was going on with us. Daddy was always blamin' Mama for everything, but this time she was blamin' Daddy. On Oct. 19, 1994, my mom, my baby's daddy, our kids, and some other family came to see us to say goodbye. I told Mama I would be okay, and that when I delivered the baby, she would have to come and get the baby 'cause it would be a long time before I could take care of her. I told my baby's daddy not to wait on me because I knew I had a lot of time in prison. I told him to just help Mama with the baby. I walked back to my cell with tears in my eyes, put my hand on my stomach, and talked to my baby. I told my unborn baby that she would make it outta prison. I stayed awake all night wonderin' what the next day was gon' be like – only God knew.

Jamie

I was scared for Gladys because I knew she had a temper. I knew we were about to come face to face with some women who wouldn't care about Gladys' temper or the baby she was carrying. For the first time in my life, I cried out for our Dad to come rescue us and he didn't - he couldn't.

~

At 5 a.m. the next morning, the sheriffs told us to get up. They brought us toast, eggs, grits, and orange juice. At 7 a.m., a female police officer came in and told us it was time to go. The day had come. We were leaving for prison – for life. We had already called to say goodbye to everybody, but we thought Daddy would come to see us off. He didn't. That "something" that had his attention must've paralyzed his mind and his body. We walked outside to the car and two officers were waiting for us with smirks on their faces. One said, "Yo daddy coulda saved y'all. Y'all gon' rot in prison and that baby goin' to the State."

Gladys

Before I knew it, I yelled, "Go to hell! All this dirty shit comin' out one day." The officer came right back and said, "When y'all dead in prison." The same officer that was makin' the ugly comments was one of the same officers that questioned us in jail on Christmas Eve. I had so much hate for the sheriff's department. I lost all respect for 'em. We hit Interstate 55 going towards Rankin County and I lit a cigarette. I remember lookin' over at Jamie and askin' her what was next. I could see she ain't have no answer for me. I knew in my heart I would never see the free world again, so I got my last good look at everything on the drive to prison. I was mad at the world. I couldn't understand how I got *two* life sentences. I was pregnant and I felt alone. I was so scared 'cause I heard a lot of stories about what happens to people in prison. I didn't want to live no more. I was havin' second thoughts about my unborn baby being with me. I didn't have no choice in the matter, but now I was scared for my baby, too.

Jamie

It was a 45 minute ride to the prison, but it seemed like it took ten minutes for us to get there. I didn't know what to expect. I didn't know what to think. I was numb with a mixture of anger and anxiety. If I had a gun the night I got to prison, I would've blown my brains out. I wasn't just terrified for myself, but I was terrified for my sister who was four months pregnant. I was so scared, I almost peed on myself. My heart was racing and felt like it was going to beat right out of my chest.

I was transported in shackles. I couldn't believe it. I thought I was dreaming. Shackles? Reality was hitting me fast and hard. I ain't never seen shackles, but I found myself wearing them. Gladys was pregnant, so she couldn't be shackled. I was happy for her because I didn't want her to feel what I was feeling wearing shackles. It was embarrassing and humiliating. I wanted to cry, but I couldn't find the tears in all my fear and anger. We arrived at the Central Mississippi Correctional Center, and we really can't say what we were thinking because we didn't know what to think. We were just scared to death. We had never been so scared in our lives. We saw a big brown building surrounded by tall barbed wire. We were at a place we never thought we'd be – prison. It was a dreary looking place. It almost looked deserted because we didn't see nobody.

The doors opened and I smelled a horrible smell. It smelled like a bunch of musty people who hadn't bathed. That smell was strong and it slapped me dead in my face like somebody punched me in the nose. I gasped for air, but all I got was a thick, dry dose of a real bad, musty odor. It was a horrible stench, and I was hoping I wouldn't have to smell it for the rest of my life.

Gladys

We was escorted through big iron doors. It didn't look deserted no more. It was a lot goin' on and a lot of people walkin' around. I wanted to know right away what my surroundings was gonna be. I needed to know what was goin' on. I saw a big glass window, so I got close enough to it to try to look through it, and a big black man yelled out, "Sit your ass down, right now!" I jumped and I swear my heart jumped outta my chest. His big ass mouth scared the shit outta me. I looked at Jamie and her eyes was full of fear. I looked at that officer and wanted to go the hell off on him, but Jamie told me to sit down and be quiet. I don't even know why he was yellin'. I didn't do nothin' but look out a damn glass window. We hadn't been there a whole hour yet, and I was ready to stir up some mess. Don't nobody yell at me like that for nothin'. I looked at Jamie and realized her head was already messed up, so I just kept my mouth closed. I was pissed.

Jamie

After we finally got finished being processed, we were taken to the shower area and it was the most humiliating thing I had ever experienced in my life. I would have rather worn shackles every day. We had to strip and take a shower with several other girls right in front of male guards. We were told we had three minutes to shower. The male guards were laughing, pointing, and yelling obscene comments at us. My mind went back to the night me and Gladys were out looking for the gas man and my car wouldn't start. The two guys were calling us names just like the prison guards were. The guards just kept pointing and laughing; I'll never forget it. I tried to ignore them, but it felt like I was being mentally raped. That wasn't the bad part.

91

After the shower, we had to bend over and spread our butt cheeks wide for the guards to look. They seemed to enjoy that, too. Words can't express how I felt, and I couldn't imagine how Gladys felt being pregnant. I kept wondering why a merciful God would allow something like this to happen to us? Why? Wasn't it enough that we were sent to prison for the rest of our lives?

Dear God, please help us! I heard one of the guards tell Gladys that her womanhood would end that day and that we belonged to the state and everybody could do what they wanted to do to us. Now, he saw that she was pregnant, but he still had the nerve to say something to her like that. I knew Gladys wanted to cuss him out, but she kept quiet for my sake. I know she did. Gladys was just as afraid for me as I was for her.

~

We couldn't understand why we were being treated so bad, but then again nobody gets sent to prison for life for $11, so we thought maybe they had it out for us from the jump. We were innocent, but nobody around us seemed to care. We hadn't done nothing wrong except follow the guards' orders and be humiliated, so why were they yelling and cussing us? We thought that maybe something was going on that we didn't know about because none of this made any sense to us. We thought we were being treated cruel, but we found out real soon that what we *thought* was cruel treatment was nothing compared to what was ahead of us.

We had to throw our own clothes in this big basket and

they gave us a yellow jump suit to put on. We also got a white pillow case with two pairs of under clothes, three white t-shirts, and two pair of socks inside. They took our pictures, fingerprinted us, and asked a lot of questions. All the paperwork was finished and we were officially identified as inmate #19197 (Jamie) and #19142 (Gladys). It wasn't long after we received our prison identification numbers that we were referred to as "The Scott Sisters."

About two hours had gone by and they brought us something to eat. Greens, bread, water, and some kind of meat we had never seen before was our first meal in prison. Neither one of us felt like eating. We picked at the food and we sure didn't eat whatever that meat was. We were used to Mama's southern, home-cooking, and the mess we saw on the plate they gave us looked like slop and tasted like something we had never tasted before.

It was our first night in prison, and we were told we were going to maximum security. Maximum security is for the trouble makers, and for inmates needing extra security or restrictions because of the level of their charge. We were bold enough to ask why we had to go to maximum security so soon, and we were told it was because of the severity of our sentence – *double* life. They wanted to make sure we wouldn't kill ourselves, so we were placed on suicide watch before they released us into the general population of the prison. We were scared out of our minds. We were yelled at, cursed at, and humiliated for no reason at all...and now we were going to maximum security.

Jamie

They really didn't have to watch me to make sure I wouldn't kill myself, I already felt dead. From the moment we walked inside the prison, my heart never stopped beating fast and hard. And poor Gladys had another heart beating inside her that nobody seemed to care about. I realized real fast that nobody cared a thing about us, or if we were innocent or not. Nobody cared that we were scared and nobody cared that we were young. I kept hoping I would wake up from this horrific nightmare. I couldn't believe this was happening to us. I cried myself to sleep my first night in prison in a 12 X 12 cell. I cried and yelled at God for letting this happen to me. Bigmama said God was a good God. Well, what in the hell was going on?

Gladys

Our walk to maximum security was outside in the rain; it was raining real hard. We had to pass by a building called the gym. It looked like it was 100 beds in that building and women was just standin' around and watchin' us walk by. We had our belongings in our hands and one woman yelled out, "What's your name? What you in here for? Y'all gon' be my bitches! I just looked and said to myself, "Over my dead body." I would fight to the end before I was anybody's bitch. I thought about all the prison movies and stories I saw and I just got more and more scared, but I wasn't about to show it. I had to be tough for me and my baby. I didn't want nothin' to happen to my baby. I had to protect my baby with everything

94

I had. It was rainin' hard, and I was cold and tired and hopin' my baby was alright.

We finally made it to the maximum security building, and was put in separate, one-man cells. The guards told us our dos and don'ts and the door was shut and locked behind us. Somethin' came over me that I can't explain. I never liked bein' cooped up and there I was locked up in prison. I felt like I was gon' suffocate. I remember lookin' around and seein' the iron bed, toilet, and face bowl. I wanted to ask somebody if I was dreamin', then I heard somebody ask me what my name was. It scared me at first 'cause I couldn't see nobody, but I know I heard somebody's voice. The voice told me to get down on the floor by the toilet and I did. I heard more voices. I heard Jamie's voice, too, and felt relieved. I didn't wanna be separated from Jamie, so when I heard her voice, I knew she was alright.

There was a vent down by the toilet and I realized that was where the voices was comin' from. The vent was how maximum security inmates talked to each other. I didn't feel like talkin', but I talked for a little while. I think I needed to know somebody else was there with me. I couldn't see nobody through the vent, but the voice let me know I wasn't by myself. We wasn't really talkin' about nothin'. The voice was just being nosey and wanted somebody to talk to.

When I finished talkin', I started to cry. I couldn't believe this was gonna be my home for the rest of my life. *Oh my God.* Nasty food, musty air, mean guards, voices from vents, and scary-lookin' women called inmates. My first night in prison was the first time I ever wanted to end my life. I cried and cried. I never cried so much in my life. I was pregnant and scared, and felt like my whole life was taken from me. Havin' my baby inside me was my only comfort. I was already pissed about goin' to prison, and then they wanna separate me from my sister and put us in maximum security? That shit didn't make no kinda sense to me. If I was gon' kill myself, I woulda killed myself *before* I got to prison. I was goin' off on one of the guards and my mouth got me in trouble. I had to stay in maximum security longer than I was s'posed to. Jamie was released from maximum security before me. Max ain't a place you wannna go to on a regular basis, but I went to Max a lot in my sixteen years in prison.

~

I guess we passed the suicide watch by not killing ourselves, so we were finally escorted to our housing area. We didn't know if it was better to be alone in maximum security or to be with the other inmates. My God! Looking at where we were going to be living for the next sixteen years took our breath away. Because we're always asked so many questions about what it's really like in prison, we decided to share details of some of our most private prison stories to give an idea of what our life was like, but not even the stories we tell can compare to being behind bars for yourself. You'll go behind bars with us and get an idea of what we felt, saw, and experienced. The things we saw in prison were things nobody could've prepared us for.

Prison life is nothing like the prison movies we saw on television or the stories we heard; television can't even compare. It's so much worse. People are ignorant to prison life just like we were. With our wildest imagination, we would have never been able to imagine life in prison. The things we experienced and saw will be with us forever. Sixteen years of our life was spent in a place where no one really cared about themselves, so naturally they didn't care about anybody else, including us. The sound of the metal bars clanking and locking behind us was worse than the knock on our door that Christmas Eve when our nightmare first started. The sounds of the rusty prison bars still ring in our heads.

We invite you behind the bars of the Central Mississippi Correctional Facility in Rankin County, Mississippi.

Jamie

I wrote a lot of stuff down that happened to us over sixteen years. I didn't keep a journal or nothing like that, but whenever I felt like I needed to write, I did. I had no idea that what I wrote would be used in a book because I really didn't expect to live to even write a book. I didn't expect to ever see beyond the prison bars – after all, I had a *double life* sentence.

SETTING THE SCENE

It's late, about 11:30 pm, and it's starting to quiet down in our housing unit. The housing unit is where we spend most of our time in prison. It's where we sleep, read and write letters, play cards, hang out, shower, use the bathroom, and whatever else we can find to do to waste the crazy amount of time we have on our hands. Everyone is pretty much going about their own business. Some are tired from working and others are tired from doing nothing at all. Everyone starts to wind down and the quietness is welcomed.

Before silence gets a chance to settle in, all of a sudden doors swing open, lights are flipped on, and strong, loud voices are yelling, "Get up, Bitches! Get up now!" The K9 unit has entered the housing unit. K9 is a group of prison guards accompanied by dogs. The dogs are beautiful to look at, but they aren't dogs to admire; they're dogs trained to kill. On command, the beauty of these dogs can turn into deadly beasts. Their sharp teeth and deep-brown, piercing eyes scare the hell out of us and we are led by pure fear to obey every instruction yelled at us by the guards.

The K9 unit is on duty just in case a riot breaks out, or if there is an escape, or something really serious happens in the prison, but every now and then they drop in unexpectedly to make our lives a little more miserable than they already are. God forbid we piss the guards or their dogs off. We know the routine, but we wait to be told what to do. No one moves a muscle without being told. After we get thoroughly cursed out by the K9 unit and they get us out of our racks, we're ordered outside the housing unit, and no matter what the weather is, we drop on the ground – face down. While we're outside, K9 is inside completely destroying our housing unit. Everything we own, which isn't much, is thrown into large garbage cans and the dogs sniff every inch of the housing unit with their sharp sense of smell. With wet, cold noses, the fierce dogs help the guards find contraband – illegal items either smuggled in or made by inmates in prison. Items like cell phones, drugs, or items that can be used as a weapon are considered contraband.

We never worried about the K9 unit finding contraband on us, but we have a precious treasure we wanted to protect – pictures. An inmate's most valuable possessions are pictures of their family and the outside world. We hang our precious photos over our racks or tape them to our lockers only to be snatched down and stomped on by K9. Each time this happens, it takes a little out of us. It feels like our hearts are being snatched out and stepped on, and it hurts like hell. Even though they're only pictures, those pictures carry us, hold us up, and give us the motivation to wake up and get through another day.

After K9 is finished destroying our housing unit, we're called back inside and escorted into the bathroom area five inmates at a time. With the men from K9 still walking around the unit, we're ordered to take off every stitch of clothing we have on. No one seems to care that we're naked while males are still in the unit. No one cares about what is going on except the inmates. Butt naked, we're ordered to squat and cough. It didn't matter if we were on our period or not, everybody had to squat and cough. We're then escorted back to our rack and made to sit on the floor facing it. We sit and watch the little property we have be destroyed some more. This whole degrading process is called a "shake-down."

K9 not only shakes our sheets, pillow, mattress, and everything we own, but they shake our peace of mind and self-worth. It seems like they want to shake it right out of us. Each shake- down is just another way to strip an inmate of any courage or willpower that may have been scraped up to get through another day. Shake-downs make us want to end our life. You would think after a few shake-downs, we would be able to shake them off and go on about our business, but they aren't something to get used to. We experienced more than our share of shake-downs in the sixteen years we spent in prison. With each passing year, we sunk deeper and deeper into hopelessness and depression. The K9 unit doesn't just destroy our stuff, they destroy us.

When shake-down is over, the inmates try to make jokes and lighten the mood, but nothing was funny about watching our kids' pictures get trampled on, ripped up, or bent like they were nothing. Pictures are all some inmates have – a memory. Nothing was funny about being exposed to a man we didn't invite to see us naked. Nothing was funny about having dogs slobber all over the racks and pillows we had to lay our head down on. None of it was funny, but we learned to laugh with the other inmates to keep from crying and losing our mind. While we pretend to laugh, the entire time we're crying inside and wishing our nightmare would end. We cried out for our daddy to rescue us from prison, but realized he wasn't coming. Nobody was coming to save us – nobody, so we prepared to live out our double life sentences in one of the most depressing looking places we'd ever seen.

Picture yourself walking into a big, empty warehouse. Now, picture rows and rows of bunk-beds, and between every fifty bunk-beds is a brick wall. Each fifty bunk-beds is called a "zone." A little section of the warehouse holds four to eight toilets that about 117 women had to share. The shower area was just as small. A single pole with a few shower heads on it was where we all rotated taking a shower, so when we took a shower, we were in a circle looking at each other.

In the middle of the warehouse was something shaped like a water tower with glass all around it that could be seen through. The tall tower was where the guards sat to watch our every move. They could also see directly into the bathroom area from the tower. Mirrors were positioned on the tower just right, so the guards could have a bird's eye view of the bathroom. They could see everything and everybody perfectly.

There was a small, 6" window by every third bed, which are actually called "racks." Each window had three bars across it and the bars were made out of 70-80 pounds of pure steel. Above the rows of bunk-beds were long vents for heat; there was no air conditioning. We need to repeat – there was NO air conditioning in our housing unit. In the summer, inmates were given big, humongous standing fans. One was placed at the head of each zone and one at the bottom of each zone. You can't even imagine how hot it got in there. Inmates fell out left and right because it got so hot. Those fans didn't blow a lick of air, and Mississippi heat ain't no joke! This big warehouse we just described was our living space for sixteen years – our housing unit. Our unusual living space was just the ice breaker for our even more unusual living conditions.

Gladys

Lookin' around at my surroundings, all I could think about was my baby growin' inside me. I kept hopin' my baby was okay. I was pissed and pregnant in prison. I knew I was gon' be uncomfortable when it got close to have my baby. The racks wasn't comfortable to sleep on at all. I think that's why they call 'em "racks," because it feels like you sleepin' on a metal rack with no mattress. I knew I wasn't in prison to be comfortable, but I wanted my baby to be okay. My baby was my main concern from the time I set foot in prison. I didn't want my baby to feel all the anger and stress I was feelin', but it was too late. I had already felt so many strong emotions and got so pissed that I don't even remember feelin' my baby move inside me. I was too occupied with what was goin' on around me to notice what was goin' on inside me. I just prayed that my baby was okay.

Bein' four months pregnant and only nineteen years old, I thought I'd get a little help in prison, but I didn't get no special treatment at all. Besides my regular prenatal exams, I was treated like all the other inmates. I woke up with the inmates, slept with 'em, worked with 'em, and I even marched with the inmates until the hour I went into labor. Thank God I ain't have no complications with my pregnancy, 'cause nobody seemed to give a damn that I was a scared, young, pregnant girl. I was just another inmate. There was women in prison a lot younger than me with worse situations, so a pregnancy was just another sad story. There wasn't no baby shower, no gifts, no cake, and no pictures. The only gift I got was a healthy baby girl and she was more than I coulda ever asked for.

Five months into our sentence, I started feelin' strong contractions. I was nervous. I knew it was time to have my baby, but wasn't sure what to do in prison, so I let one of the guards on duty know I thought I was in labor. There ain't no false labor alarms in prison, so the guard started timin' my contractions. They had to make sure I was good and ready to push before makin' a trip to the hospital. I was more than ready to push and was rushed to the hospital.

On the way to the hospital, even though I was in pain, I had a real happy feelin' about finally havin' my baby. I needed to know the little person inside me was okay, and I couldn't wait to meet and hold my newborn. Little did I know I was in for a big surprise because what was s'pose to be a happy moment for me turned into one of the shortest happy moments of my life. Right after I delivered my baby, they told me she was a girl, they cleaned me up, and took me to another room and handcuffed me to a hospital bed. They ain't even give me a chance to hold my baby girl. I wasn't just a young mother givin' birth, I was a convict givin' birth, and the guards made sure I didn't forget it. The handcuffs was s'posed to stop me from escapin'- as if I felt like runnin' somewhere after just givin' birth. Bein' handcuffed to the bed did somethin' to me. It snatched somethin' from me and I could never explain the feelings I was havin'. I carried my baby for nine months and didn't get to hold her.

It almost felt like the night I was arrested. I'll never forget that night. They put handcuffs on me like I was a criminal and took me away from my kids for no reason at all. I felt so empty that Christmas Eve, and there I was, handcuffed to a hospital bed and feelin' that same empty feelin' again and bein' snatched away from my baby. I was tired of feelin' empty. I didn't feel like goin' off on nobody. I was tired, and I was hurt. There was also two guards sittin' outside my room for extra security. I thought maybe if I asked in a nice way, they might feel sorry for me, and let me hold my baby, so I did. I asked the guards if it was possible to take the handcuffs off me for just a minute, so I could at least hold my new baby girl for a few minutes.

I couldn't believe they actually agreed to let me hold her. I anxiously watched the guards remove my handcuffs, and my newborn baby girl was brought to me, and placed in my arms. Her little warm body was like holdin' a lil' bit of joy. For just a minute, I forgot I was an inmate, and I felt like a new mom. I felt normal again, and it felt so good. Her smell gave me some comfort, and I kept my face close to hers to keep smellin' her. I remember lookin' at her small, sweet face and all of a sudden, I felt a sadness come over me. Lookin' into her eyes made me sad 'cause I knew I wasn't gon' be there to comfort her when she needed me, and the comfort she was givin' me was gon' end real soon. My baby girl had no idea that the woman holdin' her wasn't just her mom, but she was a prison inmate with a *double life* sentence.

Jamie

Gladys had her six week check-up and everything went back to normal for her, but something wasn't right with my little sister. I know my sister, and Gladys just wasn't Gladys. I didn't know exactly what it was, but I knew something wasn't right. Gladys had to return to prison with the choice of releasing her newborn baby girl to Mama or to the State. Already taking care of our other three children, Mama now had a newborn baby to take care of. Mama didn't hesitate. Just like she volunteered to take care of our first babies, she agreed to take care of this baby, too.

Gladys

Mama accepted custody of Courtney Dallas Scott. Mama wouldn't have it no other way, and me and Jamie thanked God for her. I knew Courtney would be taken care of, but it was still real hard for me to leave her. I felt like my soul was snatched away. When I got back to prison, I was angry a lot 'cause I missed out on bondin' with Courtney. That little time I got to hold her wasn't enough. I didn't feel right inside and I went off on everybody. I didn't need a reason to do it. I didn't give a damn about nobody or nothin'.

~

There are so many children of inmates being raised by the system. Not every inmate has a supportive family willing to step in and raise their kids – especially if you have a long sentence. Not every inmate has a supportive family that's financially *able* to step in and raise their kids. We met a lot of mothers in prison with life sentences and no parole. Our situation wasn't unique, which didn't make us feel no better, but we knew we weren't alone. We were more than grateful for our mother being available *and* able to take care of our kids. The fathers of our kids didn't offer no kind of support. They weren't even in contact with the kids the whole time we were in prison. They basically disappeared, which wasn't surprising to us. Daddy stepped in and was a father to our kids. Our kids called their granddad "Daddy."

Gladys

I was in love with Courtney's father. He was the first man I loved with all my heart. He was my best friend and I felt like my goin' to prison destroyed my only chance of true love. I told him when I left not to wait, and he sho' didn't. I don't blame him. I probably wouldn't wait for nobody with a double life sentence either.

Jamie

I was happy that I didn't have contact with my baby daddies because I didn't want them trying to take my kids from my parents. I got pregnant by three sorry men, and I didn't expect them to do nothing anyway. Mama always sent us pictures of Courtney and the other kids, but nothing could take the place of seeing our family in person. Seeing their faces gave us strength. We saw our family every other week, but the visits always went by real fast; they were never long enough.

~

We were always a tight-knit family, so being separated from our family took some getting used to. It was tough, and it was even tougher to be separated from our kids; they were so young. At least we weren't separated from each other and we knew, as sisters, we had each other's back. The tight bond we had as little girls paid off. We were still two peas in a pod, but we became two peas in prison. We *had* to be there for each other. We had to strengthen each other, encourage each other, and hold each other up. We stuck by each other the best we could. As we got used to our new, unusual environment in the big warehouse-looking building, we realized our bond is what kept us strong. There was nothing familiar about our surroundings except each other, so we stuck together like glue.

As the days, weeks, and months rolled by, we started getting used to the big warehouse that became our home. We started to meet other inmates and get to know some of their names and the names of some of the guards. Some of the inmates were nice and others not so nice. A lot of them had hidden motives and others were down-to-earth, good people. We didn't have nothing to offer anybody, but as time went on and we got to know the prison system, we found out that and we got to know the prison system, we found out that everybody in prison had *something* that somebody else wanted. We saw things behind bars that were ten times worse than what we saw from our bedroom window in Chicago.

With so much time on our hands sitting in prison, our minds would always go back to when Daddy was so protective of us. We didn't want his protection then, but while we were in prison, we wished we had our Daddy's protection, and we especially wished he could've protected us from going to prison in the first place. But Daddy seemed to be in his own secret prison. We wondered if Daddy needed protection from somebody or something. We couldn't help Daddy, and he couldn't help us. Sometimes, we even wondered if he *wanted* to help us because it didn't seem like it. Sitting in prison makes you think a lot of crazy stuff, and we knew Daddy loved us and would've done anything to help us, but we couldn't help the thoughts that kept coming to our minds. *Why, Daddy? Why?*

We witnessed some horrifying things in prison that we couldn't do nothing about. We saw guards physically and sexually abuse inmates – the same guards that were supposed to be protecting us. How in the hell were we supposed to trust these guards? They threatened to hurt us if we said *anything* about what we saw. Who in the world were we supposed to call for help? *Dear God, please help us!*

We knew we had the rest of our lives in prison, and sexual abuse seemed to be a routine practice. We were told to get used to it. Get used to it? We couldn't even get used to being locked up! We stayed in a state of shock everyday as we witnessed what was happening behind bars that nobody seemed to care about. How do you get used to sexual abuse and why wasn't it being reported? For sixteen years, we witnessed rapes, fights, suicides, and beatings, but were never able to "get used to it." It wasn't just guards against inmates, but it was also inmates against inmates. We couldn't win either way. Some inmates found a way to "get used to" the abuse and even learned how to use the abuse to their benefit.

As sad as it sounds, instead of being raped or abused, some inmates chose to sell their bodies for things they either wanted or needed. Things like a bar of soap, face cream, or whatever they felt like they needed to survive was given in exchange for sexual favors. The mindset was, if they had to give up their bodies, it was going be on their terms. Again, we were in shock. We were being exposed to a life we knew nothing about. Even the horrific fist fights between our parents didn't compare to what we were seeing.

Visits from our family was really the only normalcy we had in prison. We looked forward to visiting hours because it took us away from the reality of life in the big warehouse. Visiting hours in prison were priceless, but eventually, even that changed for us, too. We remember one of the very first visits. Mama, Daddy, our big sister Boonanie, and our kids came and stayed for about three hours. Mama cried and so did we. We held our kids and cried some more. We tried to take mental pictures that would hold us over until the next visit, but those mental pictures wasn't the same as seeing their faces in person.

Daddy always just sat close by with his head down. We figured he couldn't handle seeing us locked up. From the day the jury found us guilty, Daddy just wasn't Daddy. He wasn't the same. We knew Daddy to be strong and courageous, but he seemed to have turned into a helpless and hopeless man. We weren't used to seeing Daddy with his head down all the time. Daddy used to look everybody dead in their eyes, but it didn't even seem like he could barely look at us at all, and he definitely couldn't look us in our eyes anymore. That first prison visit was the last time we saw Daddy for a long, long time. He accepted all our phone calls and sent us money, but Daddy completely stopped coming to see us. We didn't understand it; it didn't make any sense to us. We knew Daddy was taking us going to prison harder than anyone, but we never thought he'd stop visiting us. It was five years before we saw Daddy again – a whole five years. He didn't tell us why he didn't come visit, but we had an idea.

Daddy couldn't handle seeing us sitting in prison. We thought he might've felt responsible for us being locked up. After all, he was Daddy - he was our protector, and we were his girls. We wondered if Daddy was, in fact, responsible for us going to prison. Mama had always blamed him, but Mama blamed Daddy for a lot of stuff that happened to us; they blamed each other. After those long five years without any visits from our protector, all of a sudden Daddy showed up again and started coming to see us on a regular basis. We were happy to see Daddy, but every time the visits were over, he would get up, say goodbye, and not look back at us. Daddy *never* looked back at us to wave, to smile, or just to take another look at us, his girls. *Why, Daddy? Why?*

Five years after the alleged armed robbery happened, a guy that worked in the prison thought enough about us to tell us about a highly-respected crime lawyer in Mississippi named Chokwe Lumumba. We called home and told Daddy about him. Without hesitation, Daddy contacted Attorney Lumumba, and set an appointment to meet with him. Daddy was obviously impressed with him, because Mr. Lumumba became our new attorney. We believed we found a good lawyer, and we were so happy and relieved to know we had another chance to prove our innocence. Our hope was rekindled.

Just because time was passing us by while we were sitting in prison, we never once accepted our guilty verdict. We knew we were innocent, but being behind bars for a long time can make an innocent inmate think they're supposed to be there. Prison life became our life, but we always had hope that somebody, somewhere would rescue us.

Attorney Lumumba immediately dived into our case, fought for us, and filed an appeal. He contacted the second co-defendant in our case, who didn't testify in court, and got the co-defendant to agree to sign an affidavit stating we had nothing to do with the armed robbery. When we heard the news, we knew we had the right lawyer. We knew the signed affidavit would be another chance for us to prove our innocence. We didn't know what an affidavit was, but quickly found out what it meant and what it meant to us. We learned a lot about the court system, but unfortunately, it was all at the expense of our freedom while we sat behind bars.

The appeal was denied. Attorney Lumumba also petitioned the governor of Mississippi, Governor Barbour, for commutation of our sentence; it was also denied. We didn't really understand what commutation was either, but we knew it meant an exchange for a lesser sentence than what we were serving. We didn't want to be in prison at all, but would have gladly taken a lesser sentence than *double life*. We didn't understand. Where was the justice? We couldn't believe this was *really* happening in the United States of America. We were nineteen and twenty-one years old and we each received a *double life* sentence for $11 dollars. Was justice served? If so, to who?

Mr. Lumumba was a mild, gentle person, but when he got in court, he was a raging bull. We had faith in him. He continued to fight for our freedom while we sat in prison day after day, month after month. Attorney Lumumba gave us new hope. We were just happy that someone thought enough about us to not let us rot away in prison, and some days that is exactly what it felt like – like we were rotting away. There were times we felt like Attorney Lumumba was the only person working for us, but we later realized there was a whole team of people behind us. This was good to know, because nobody was trying to help us from inside the prison. There was no help to be found in prison.

Nobody goes to prison to make friends, and we learned real fast that it's best to not trust nobody. Sometimes our hearts wanted to trust, but we knew better, and every day was a struggle with our emotions. We realized that even though we were in a building full of women, we were still alone. Besides trusting each other, we were hesitant about growing close to anybody else. Everybody in prison had a game or a motive to get something out of you. You would think people in prison would have each other's back since we're all locked up, but that wasn't the case at all. As sisters, we had each other's back, and we depended on *only* each other.

We had a double life sentence, so we had plenty of time to get to know other inmates. We slowly started to connect with them and found ourselves slowly listening to our hearts instead of our minds. There was really no way around it – human nature had its way. As hard as we tried to stay to ourselves, our new life in prison was surrounded by a bunch of women 24/7 – women who had little contact with the outside world, women who were lonely, some falsely accused, women with no family support, and women looking for someone to have their back. We did everything with these women. We slept, ate, showered, cleaned and complained with them. We had something in common with these women – we were all convicts. We found out real fast that there was no such thing as staying to yourself in prison. When you set yourself apart from the other inmates, you set yourself up to be a target for a whole lot of mess.

We being friendly and building relationships would help the time go by faster. We reluctantly let our guards down and friendships started to form with the women in our housing unit – the big warehouse. We spent time with them – convicts. We helped them, supported them, cried with them, and if needed, we protected them – convicts. We were in prison, but it was hard to consider ourselves as convicts. As far as we were concerned, we were in prison *with* convicts. We weren't supposed to be there, but everybody else was. No doubt, a lot of convicts around us probably looked at us the same way we looked at them...as convicts. Surprisingly to us, we actually found a few inmates we felt comfortable enough to call friends.

Time passed, and before we knew it, we were bonding with our newfound friends - convicts. There were plenty other inmates who violated our trust, stole from us, and lied on us or to us, but we learned to stick with our small circle of friends. These friends, convicts, became our new family - our family behind bars. We started to depend on our new family, and just like Daddy taught us, we were there for our family. We had their back, too. If they needed something, we did our best to make sure they had it. We didn't have the freedom to run to a corner store if something was needed, in prison we had something called "Canteen."

Prison canteen was like the prison's shopping network. Once a week, inmates who had money in their prison account could order from a list of items like food, snacks, hygiene products, and underwear. Within a few days after ordering, clear plastic bags were delivered with the ordered items inside. Canteen delivery day was like waiting for the UPS truck to arrive with a package. Although the canteen items cost twice as much as they did in a regular store, we looked forward to the only form of shopping we had behind bars. Not all inmates were able to afford canteen shopping, but

114

Daddy made sure we always had money in our prison account. He made a deposit on a regular basis, and sometimes we had enough in our account to help out a few of our friends who didn't have support from their family.

Again, having a supportive family is so important to an inmate, and it even makes prison time a little more tolerable – just a little. Outside support was our lifeline to the world – the free world. Inmates without canteen privileges felt hopeless and would manipulate other inmates to get what they wanted. We saw this happen over and over, and it made us grateful for Daddy making sure we never got to the point to have to ask another inmate for help, or be desperate enough to start being manipulative like other inmates were being. We learned how to ration in prison; we had to. If we ran out of something, we had to wait for our next scheduled issue of supplies or wait for canteen delivery.

Toilet tissue was one of the most important items we had to ration. We don't know who came up with the numbers, but we were issued two rolls of one-ply toilet tissue a week, one bar of odorless soap, and eight sanitary napkins. We also got one tube of clear toothpaste a month, which wasn't just used for the obvious, but it was used for glue and whatever inmates could come up with. These items were treasured items in prison, but the two rolls of toilet tissue were like gold. If we ran out, we knew not to try to borrow from nobody else. If we were in desperate need of some, we paid two or three dollars for a roll. If inmates didn't have the money, they were just S.O.L.

We never knew which day of the week our supplies would

come in, so we rationed and conserved like we were on a desert island. It made no sense at all, but toilet paper wasn't on the canteen list. It was a hot item on the prison black market. This was just another way to make the life of an inmate a living hell. If you don't think so, try to use only two rolls of one–ply toilet paper in a week. It sounds easy, but try it without using any other paper products in your house like paper towels, napkins, or Kleenex. Take all those away, and then see how easy it is. We bet you'll have a greater appreciation for paper products – especially toilet tissue.

Toilet tissue brings on another issue we had to get used to in prison. Privacy. There was no such word in prison. Modesty? To our surprise, it eventually faded away, too. That first night, when we got to prison and had to shower and be humiliated in front of male guards, should've been a clue to what our privacy or lack of privacy was gonna be like. Toilets aren't even two feet away from each other, so someone will always be close enough to smell, hear, and watch you pee or do your other business. Our days of going to the bathroom, shutting the door, and doing number two in private disappeared. If this isn't humiliating enough, think about having to wipe yourself or change a bloody sanitary napkin in front of a bunch of other women.

There was no privacy in prison – period. Everyone knows when your cycle starts, how long it stays on, and when it stops. It's no secret when you have diarrhea, are constipated, or have gas either. Everything was open and free to the general public – literally speaking. Showers were no different. You always had someone standing next to you or across from you when you showered. This can be a very emotional time for women who are shy or feel uncomfortable dressing or undressing in front of other people, but prison will break you of every bashful bone in your body.

Prison broke us of a lot of things. New inmates have a hard time getting used to a life behind bars; we sure did. We heard a lot of sniffling and saw a lot of tears in prison. We cried a lot and wiped a lot of tears, too. Inmates who had been there for a long time and had a heart would try to help the new inmates, but there were some inmates who would tell you to suck it up and shut the hell up. As our days, months, and years passed, sometimes it helped just to have someone with you while you cried. It wasn't a thing another inmate could do to help, but just being there helped a lot.

We realized that just because we were locked up didn't mean our problems, from the outside world, would go away. We were young, so we didn't have the problems a lot of other inmates had. Our main problem was the fact that we were behind bars and weren't supposed to be. That was *our* problem! We met inmates with money problems, family problems, marriage or relationship problems, health problems, and anything else you could think of. *Everybody* had a problem.

Not being able to do nothing about the problems only made inmates mad, but we were already mad at the world before we got to prison. We were mad because of the justice system. We were mad at law enforcement, and anyone else we thought of that we could be mad at. Sometimes, we got so mad that crying was the only outlet we had. It wasn't like we could go for a walk or go to another room to be alone. The best we could do was to just lay on our racks and cry.

We've been told that tears cleanse and heal, so we should be healed of any and every illness, disease, and heartbreak we'll ever have because we cried a lot of tears in sixteen years. We had some moments that brought us happy tears also, but nowhere near as often as the sad tears. It's hard to believe we actually had good times in prison, but prison became our home and the inmates became our family. We remember a few of those so-so happy times.

Jamie

I was walking to the kitchen one day minding my own business and all of a sudden, my pants fell down to the ground. I don't know if I didn't have them tight enough or what, but they fell straight down off my behind. I laughed so hard I cried, and almost wet myself. I will never forget how good it felt to laugh. I was in a dark situation, but it felt good to feel and hear myself laugh. It reminded me that I was a human being with emotions other than anger. My laugh reminded me that I was alive. I didn't know if I was laughing because my pants fell down or if I was laughing to keep from crying. I really didn't care, and didn't think too hard about it, I just enjoyed being happy in that short moment. That day, I learned joy could be found in *any* situation. When your pants fall down, pull them up and keep going.

Gladys

I had a friend that would cook on my birthday and, 'cause everybody knew I loved to dance, my friend would get another inmate to put on a little dance show for me. My birthday was special to me, and dancin' brought me a lot of happiness and laughter. In prison, you had to find ways to get through the day and try to support each other. You had to find ways to keep from feelin' like you were losin' your mind. Knowin' somebody cared enough about me to try to make my day better was like healin' to me. It was like they helped me find my way through a dark tunnel, and we had a lot of dark tunnels to go through. Laughter really is good medicine. It was damn good medicine in prison, and it kept me sane.

~

It's rare to meet an inmate who was always upbeat and happy, but we had the pleasure of meeting one named, Angie. Angie was black as night and wore bright red lipstick. She was a naturally happy person and being an inmate didn't suffocate her happiness. Angie was different. She was *always* dancing and singing. The guards knew she would never hurt anyone, so whenever she wanted to go outside to sing and dance, or just to get some fresh air, she was always allowed to. Angie was in prison for burning her father's house down, but her father visited her faithfully.

One day, a guard put Angie in maximum security. None of the inmates could imagine what Angie could've done, if anything, to be put in maximum security. Angie never bothered nobody and she wasn't a trouble-maker. Some stupid guard probably put her in Max because they didn't like seeing her happy. Some of the guards were mean just for the sake of being mean. While she was in Max, some of us would sneak by Angie's window from the outside and talk with her. We felt so bad for Angie.

Jamie

One day, I went by Angie's window, yelled out her name and she didn't answer, which was unusual for her. A few minutes later, there was a ruckus around the maximum security unit and I heard one of the other Max inmates yell, "Angie's dead!" I heard what was said, but didn't want to believe it. Unfortunately, it was true. Angie had hung herself. I couldn't believe it, and I cried like a baby. I knew Angie killed herself because she couldn't handle being caged. She was full of life and joy. She needed to be free – as free as prison would let her be. The system broke Angie's spirit and everyone's spirit she touched. She gave so many inmates happiness and hope, and when she left us, she took some of that happiness and hope with her. I always feared that Gladys would end up hurting herself in prison because she had always hated being locked up and cooped up. I'm so thankful she never did.

Never Going Home

Angie's death made us wonder if we would ever get to the point where we didn't just *wish* we were dead, but would actually do something about it. Because we had a double life

120

sentence, we knew we would eventually die in prison, but we still had a little hope. We didn't want to have false hope, but at the same time we wanted to live in reality, and at least try to accept our severe and unjust prison sentence. We weren't hearing positive news from our team of lawyers and nothing seemed to be going right. Everything done on our behalf was either denied, rejected, or ignored, so we accepted prison as our home – to live and die. We had to eventually face the fact that we would never be going home. As hard as it was, we had to accept that we would die behind bars from old age – or by taking our own life like Angie did.

Jamie

I had a life sentence, so it was time to get comfortable. Not life, but *double life.* I tried my best to stop focusing on going home and just focus on my life in prison. As soon as I accepted my double life sentence, I had a strange dream. In my dream, I saw the prison doors swing wide open, and someone was on the other side of the doors saying, "Come on!" That dream was so real that I actually found a little hope inside of me. I woke up the next morning believing I wasn't going to die in prison. I did my best to remember that dream and focus on it when my days seemed to be the darkest.

Gladys

I made up in my mind that I was gon' die in prison way before Angie took her life. What else was I s'pose to do with a double life sentence? I was ready to fight my way out, but after a while, I got tired of fightin', and I didn't think nobody on the outside was fightin' for my freedom. After a lot of nights feelin' so depressed and hopeless, I remembered Bigmama's talks about Jesus. I knew God didn't want me in prison for the rest of my life, so I kept the hope and faith my Bigmama told me about. I tried my best not to focus on gettin' out of prison, but to just do my time... one day at a time – for a lifetime.

Less Than Minimum Wage

Working while we were in prison was something else to help pass the time away and keep our sanity. To sit around day after day doing nothing but watching T.V., sleeping, fussing and fighting, or playing spades will drive you out of your mind. Taking one day at a time took way too much time, so we worked to help pass the minutes and hours away.

Jamie

I tutored inmates for their GED and also worked as a tour guide. Churches would bring their young adults in, and I would talk to them about prison life and how bad choices could lead to prison. The system had almost convinced me that I was in prison for making bad choices, but I kept telling myself I was innocent. I wanted to tell those young adults that I was in prison by mistake, and that I wasn't supposed to be there. I wanted to tell them that I was wrongly convicted. I wanted to tell them the truth, but instead, I played the role of a convict and did my job. The pay in prison was pennies, but I enjoyed talking to the young people that came. I always wanted to be in a position to give young people counsel, but never thought it would be from the inside of a prison.

Gladys

Six weeks after I had Courtney, I started workin' like a Hebrew slave. I worked anywhere I was allowed to work. I had to in order to keep my mind right. I was a tutor for a program called industry sewing. I can sew almost anything and I can sew good – real good. I also worked in the kitchen helpin' to get meals ready. I helped unload trucks of food, I worked inside, outside, and wherever they let me. I worked a lot and I worked hard. I tried to get lost in my work to keep my mind off my situation. I always tried to work real long and hard during the day, so I would be so tired in the evening, and hopefully get to sleep at night.

~

Because of the crazy things that happen in prison, we rarely got a good, sound sleep. Not getting sleep or the proper rest over so many years, plus the stress of being locked up, will make an inmate age real fast. There was always something going on in prison – always. There were always inmates arguing and fighting, metal bars closing and opening, and guards yelling and harassing inmates for no reason. Guards were also known to approach inmates late at night for sexual favors. If you had already been approached by a midnight creeping guard, you can almost guarantee that guard would be back to visit you. A lot of inmates try to stay awake at night hoping and praying the guards would pass by their bunk and give their body a break. Some inmates take pills to sleep during the day because they don't sleep at night.

Since we've been released, we still have sleepless nights. We both have nightmares about our sixteen years in prison and the things we saw and experienced. We wake up at two and three o'clock in the morning in cold sweats. There are nights we wake up crying and, sometimes, screaming. We always have nightmares of the sexual and mental abuse we heard and experienced. We dream about prison, but the one good thing about our sleepless nights is that they are now sleepless beyond the bars and not behind the bars. We awake from our nightmares in a bed instead of on a hard rack. We awake from our nightmares behind a locked door and not heavy, steel doors. We can look around and be thankful we aren't waking up in prison. We haven't had a good night's sleep since we first entered prison at ages nineteen and twenty-one.

Gladys

Sometimes I feel like I am mentally destroyed. I'll never forget prison life. Some nights, I have to take somethin' to help me sleep because I have trouble fallin' asleep on my own and even when I take somethin', I sometimes still have problems sleepin'. There are a lot of mornings that I wake up around 4:30 – 5:00 in the mornin', wide awake and not able to go back to sleep.

~

All the long, hard-working hours and the sleepless nights took a toll on our physical bodies, but just because we were locked up didn't mean we didn't want to look and feel nice. We were still young ladies, and a little lipstick goes a long way in prison. Makeup really wasn't a want, but a need to help us get through the day. It's easy to let yourself go and not care about yourself in prison. All the verbal abuse and name calling was enough to strip us of the little self-esteem we had, so a little makeup went a long way.

Having a nice hair style would make us feel better, so we were happy hair products and makeup were sold on the canteen. If we wanted to get our hair done, a list would go around for us to sign and we paid eight dollars, which came out of our prison account. Again, that family support meant everything to us. If no one was sending inmates money, they didn't get their hair done, and just did the best they could with their hair on their own. There was a cosmetology school on the prison grounds, so the women who graduated would do our hair. They had some skills!

Every inmate dealt with being imprisoned in their own way and everybody had different coping skills. Some worked, some tried to sleep their time away, some fought and argued, some read, and some would depend on a little red lipstick, but out of all the things inmates did to keep from losing their minds, smoking was at the top of the list. Out of all the wants, needs, and desires in prison, cigarettes were the most powerful. Cigarettes played a big part in getting contraband behind bars. You can buy jewelry, clothes, and even drugs with a pack or two of cigarettes. Cigarettes can get an inmate almost anything except freedom. Cigarettes can buy an inmate's deepest prison desires, and can even buy physical protection.

Most of the inmates in prison were smokers, so cigarettes were well overpriced on the canteen. For heavy chain smokers, a carton of cigarettes was worth everything they had. If canteen delivery was late one week, which was a lot, cigarettes could be sold for almost any price. It was like the "Let's Make a Deal" game show. Inmates would sell a precious pack of noodles for two cigarettes, and noodles were popular because they saved us from having to eat the kitchen's nasty, bland food for at least one night. As for the non-smokers, they could have anything they wanted just by supplying the deadly addiction of nicotine-driven inmates.

Gladys

I was one of those nicotine-driven inmates. I started smokin' when I was thirteen years old. I would steal Mama and Daddy's cigarettes. I thought I was cute and grown smokin' at thirteen, but I got my butt beat many times for gettin' caught smokin'. I could never figure out why my parents beat me for smokin' when they smoked right in front of us. Since they was doin' it, I thought it was okay for me to take a puff every now and then, too.

When I first got to prison, I started smokin' a lot more – a

126

whole lot more. I went from a half a pack a day to two packs a day. I would run out of cigarettes a lot in prison, but people knew not to talk to me or mess with me until I got some more. You didn't want to be around me if I ran out of cigarettes. I tried my best to always keep some, but it was hard 'cause cigarettes helped me release pressure and stress, and I was *always* stressed. So I kept a cigarette lit, and I mean I *kept* a cigarette lit. Cigarettes can get you killed or hurt in prison. It's that bad. Smokin' calmed me down a lot, but it probably didn't seem like it 'cause I was always fightin' and in trouble. Nobody knew what was goin' on in my mind. Cigarettes was a life-saver for me in prison. They calmed me down a whole lot.

Since I been out of prison, I tried to stop smokin', but the habit is hard to break – it's real hard. People try to get me to stop, but again, don't nobody know what I dealt with for sixteen years behind bars and they don't know what I still deal with in my head. Like I said, smokin' in prison helped me release pressure and stress, and it calmed me down a whole lot. I ain't in prison, but I still deal with a lot of pressure and stress in my life. Smokin' is a hard habit to break.

Jamie

Smoking wasn't my problem. I never smoked, but I had another habit. I didn't commit armed robbery, but while I was in prison, I became a thief. I stole food from the kitchen all the time to take back to my unit – this is how I survived. I would take anything I could find to make a small meal. The kitchen food wasn't consumable most of the time. I was probably just spoiled from Mama's home-cooking, but from the first night in prison when I had my first meal, I knew I was in trouble. The food was nasty from day one. Half the time, I couldn't make out what it was that I was supposed to be eating...and I refused to go hungry.

Sometimes I would get caught, but offering the guards a soda or something would sometimes free me from the consequences. I know stealing don't support my innocence in my case for armed robbery, but I think there is a difference in being accused of armed robbery for $11 and taking food out of a prison kitchen. I know stealing is stealing regardless of the situation, and I admit stealing from the prison kitchen, but I will *never* admit to the armed robbery I've been accused of. I'll go to my grave maintaining my innocence. I did *not* commit armed robbery.

Eating was my stress reliever, and I was hungry. Guards knew what I was doing, and inmates knew guards could be paid off for almost anything. The sad part about stealing in prison was that the prison staff would often ask inmates to steal supplies for them, so they wouldn't have to purchase the products themselves. The staff *asked* us to steal for them! So, stealing was okay as long as the prison staff benefitted? What kind of sense did that make? If you didn't come in prison corrupt, you had a good chance of leaving corrupt if your head wasn't right.

~

There were plenty other hungry inmates in prison who

refused to eat the prison food, which is why Ramen Noodles were so popular with inmates. Noodles, like cigarettes, were a hot commodity in prison. We had something called Toilet Noodles, which helped support our out-of-control desperation to eat a good, hot meal. The directions for Ramen Noodles are simple: open the package, empty contents into a bowl, add water, microwave a few minutes, and add the seasoning packet. Easy, right? What if you don't have a microwave?

Well, behind bars are two shiny appliances called a toilet and a sink. The sink doesn't run hot water, but the toilet has a strong flushing force. The toilets in prison flush like no toilet we've ever seen before. Every time the toilet is flushed, the water gets hotter. If you flushed the toilet over and over while you sat on it, you'd probably burn your behind. A hungry inmate must have figured out how to use the prison appliances to make hot noodles, because the word got out and having hot noodles is no longer a problem in prison.

The canteen sold large, clear cups and we used them for a lot of different things – one was for heating up our noodles. We took one of those cups and filled it with water from the sink. Then, we flushed the toilet about ten times. On the last flush, we stuck the cup in the hole at the bottom of the toilet and let the hot water fill up around the cup. We took the cup out of the toilet and put our noodles in the cup of hot water and we had some good ole hot noodles in about three to five minutes. The cup came with a lid, but because the water level in the toilet didn't quite reach the top of the cup, we didn't need the lid. Yeah, it sounds nasty. Our prison recipe for

Toilet Noodles doesn't sound appetizing, but in prison you learn to exhaust your resources. The hot water from the toilet was the next best thing to a microwave.

When it comes to food, inmates are no different from people in the free world. Inmates love to eat and we love comfort food – as comforting as it can be in prison. Sometimes we went to extreme measures to satisfy food cravings. One of the most popular prison comfort foods was a grilled cheese sandwich. Some of the best grilled cheese sandwiches were made with an iron. We didn't use the same iron we ironed our uniforms with, but we had an iron set aside just for those hot, cheesy sandwiches.

With a little cheese and bread that somebody would take from the kitchen and a warm iron, you can have cheesy comfort in no time. We had to make sure we held the iron at just the right angle and that it was on just the right temperature so we didn't burn ourselves or the sandwich. Those irons made good salmon cakes, too. God forbid you ever have to go to prison. But if you do, and you get hungry, you know what to do.

It was rare that an inmate got disciplined for stealing food because there were a lot of other things that were a whole lot worse to get in trouble for. Max wasn't the name of a guard or an inmate. Max was short for "Maximum Security," which is where Angie committed suicide and where we spent our first night in prison. Some inmates will spend the rest of their lives in these tiny cells with few chances to smell fresh air. Max is solitary confinement. Inmates in Max have nothing but their own imaginations to keep them company. Max is used to house inmates who might be a threat to themselves or to others. Inmates with too many write-ups (referrals), plus those who are labeled mentally incompetent, are housed in Max – which only adds to an inmate's misery. Death Row inmates are housed in Max also, but no one really knows who they are because they have *never* been in the general population of the prison.

Max is a lonely place, and you can easily lose your mind if you have to stay there for a long time. You only get to shower 2-3 times a week, and this is if you and the other inmates in your zone have been on good behavior, which doesn't happen a lot. When Max inmates get bored, they get real creative and think of crazy stuff. Max inmates have been known to pee in their only drinking cup and throw their urine through the narrow slot in the door. Prison guards or inmates don't really want to work in the maximum security area for that and so many other reasons. It's a sad place. We know because we were introduced to Max on more than one occasion – beginning with our first night in prison.

Gladys

I spent a lot of time in Max – too much time. My mouth sent me to Max. I didn't bite my tongue for nobody and guards don't like smart-mouth inmates. My first ten years in prison, I didn't do nothin' but fight. I didn't take nothin' from nobody. I knew fightin' would send me right to lockdown in Max security, but I didn't give a damn. If I had to fight, I fought and I dealt with the punishment that was comin' to me. I'm short, but I can hold my own with no problem. I guess I got my fightin' spirit from Mama.

Jamie

I only had one fight, and only went to Max a few times out of the sixteen years I was in prison... unlike Gladys, who made Max her second home. I wasn't a trouble-maker and tried my best to stay out of everybody's way. One night, I heard that these girls were going to wait 'til I was asleep and rob me of the little I had. I'm glad somebody told me what was supposed to go down because I got ready. I put some canned goods in my pillow case and waited for them to come; I was ready.

When they got close enough to me, I swung that pillow case as hard as I could. I swung it like a crazy woman and hit one of the girls. The other girl got out of the way. After that, they left me alone and I never had any trouble. I guess they had to try me since I was usually quiet and kept to myself. Since Gladys was always fighting, they probably wanted to see what I was made of.

After that incident, the inmates started respecting me. I was quiet, but I wasn't about to let nobody bully me. Sometimes, it just takes one time to fight back for people to leave you alone. I never got sent to Max for fighting, but I did get sent for cussing a guard out. Although I was quiet natured, sometimes I just got tired of being mistreated, cussed out, and abused for no reason at all. I would let stuff build up inside me and explode. Unfortunately, I exploded on the wrong person, a guard, and was sent to Max.

Crafty Convicts

So many inmates got sent to Max for possession of illegal items like cell phones, drugs, guns, and knives that aren't even allowed in prison, but guards found them all the time. These illegal items are called "contraband," and contraband doesn't just walk in prison on its own, or magically appear under somebody's rack. There are inmates who are expert manipulators and know exactly how to con prison officials to get exactly what they want. It happens; we saw it for ourselves. There are some real sneaky people in prison. Some inmates can convince the guards to do whatever they want them to do. The problem with this is that these officers let certain inmates get away with anything and everything.

Guards showing favoritism was something real common in prison, and they didn't care if other inmates knew about it. They definitely didn't care if other inmates told the administration. The officers who really care and want inmates to be protected and rehabilitated are few and far between. Eventually, those officers who were helping to smuggle the contraband in were set up and exposed by other officers. Some were charged with felonies and ended up on the opposite side of the bars that they worked on. It must've been hell for them to have to be in prison with the same inmates they mistreated. Who will *they* call for help? It's sad when someone is in a position of authority over a group of law-breakers and they end up breaking the law themselves. You'd think they'd know better. Who's really the prisoner? Crooked morals breed crooked guards, and crooked guards create a crooked system.

Inmates weren't only master manipulators, but a lot of them were experts at the art of escaping. We're not talking about literally escaping from prison, but mentally escaping from the demoralizing prison environment. It's easy to get bored in prison, so we learned the game of mental escape quickly. One of the safest ways to escape without getting in trouble was to read. Reading was better than fighting over what to watch on television, sleeping, or losing another card game of Spades. Even if you didn't like to read, being bored in prison made an inmate look for some type of escape in a magazine, a book, or anything that would temporarily arrest your mind.

Gladys

There was always talk about bustin' out of prison. Every inmate thought about escapin', but nobody ever got away with it. Readin' was one of my favorite ways to escape, but the books I was readin' was stuff that didn't help my brain at all. The stuff I was readin' didn't really give me no wisdom or knowledge. It didn't help my mind improve at all, but at least I was readin'. There wasn't no decent magazines in prison to help us stay up on what was goin' on in the world, so I read what was there: romance novels and trashy erotica books.

Every now and then, I would come across a good book, like a novel, but they wasn't as good as the juicy romance novels that fed my wild imagination.

The bad part about escapin' was comin' back to reality. No matter where or how I escaped, I had to come back to my real world of double life in prison. The fantasy world I was readin' about was a lot better than my reality. Pretendin' to be another person in another place was like a short break outside the prison walls. I probably didn't read what I shoulda been readin', but a lot of times, it kept me from fightin' or feelin' frustrated and confused in my mind. Callin' somebody in the free world always helped me escape, too, but that was too expensive.

~

We didn't have cell phones in prison, but we had telephone privileges from seven to ten o'clock every morning. It was like having a cell phone, but only being able to use it for three hours a day and then having to turn it off until the next day. We would stand in line for hours hoping to get a chance to talk to friends, family, lawyers, or anyone who would accept a collect call. Phone hours were the next best thing to visiting hours, but there was one big difference. Phone privileges were real expensive, so we couldn't afford to call every day like we wanted to. We didn't have to pay for the calls, but the person accepting that collect call on the other end was paying for it. We knew minutes were money, so we tried our best to use them wisely.

The system robs the families of inmates with those high-priced prison calls, so we had to save some of those phone calls for when we *really* needed to make a call. You never know when you'll need to make an emergency call and desperately need the person on the other end of the phone to say, "Yes, I'll accept." Sometimes, an emergency was just desperation to talk to someone you loved and missed so much. Hearing the voices of our kids and parents helped us get through rough moments. If they didn't accept the call, it didn't always mean they didn't want to talk to you, but maybe they couldn't afford to keep accepting high-priced collect calls. We never had a problem with our family accepting our calls. Daddy *always* accepted our calls.

Mama did her part to help us cope with being locked up, too, and nothing made a day brighter than getting mail and receiving a package from Mama. Mail call was like Christmas when we received packages, and canteen delivery day didn't come close to getting those care packages from home. To be honest, a package from anyone would have made our day, but Mama's packages were wrapped and filled with love. She would send us snacks, perm kits for our hair, and other little items she thought would help to brighten our day. It really didn't matter what was in the package, because just knowing Mama was thinking about us meant the world to us.

Boxes couldn't be larger than 13x13 and couldn't weigh over 15 pounds. Unfortunately, that size was more than large enough for a few contraband items to be easily smuggled in, and that's exactly what started happening. All it took was for a few inmates to receive drugs in the 13x13 packages and our mail call for packages ended. A few inmates ruined a good thing for the rest of us. The package privileges ended in 2004, but we could still receive letters.

When our case became known across the country, we started getting letters from supporters from all over the world. We couldn't believe it. This uplifted and encouraged us in ways we could never explain. We received so much mail on a daily basis that the mail room would deliver our mail to us in big bundles. It was overwhelming to us, but in a good way. It brought tears to our eyes to know we weren't forgotten.

We felt so much love from people we didn't even know; they gave us new hope! Some of our most cherished letters were from children, and we still have some of those letters. Letters go a long way in prison. Every day, inmates look forward to mail call and hope their name is called. Letters let us know somebody took time out of their day to sit down and write us. Letters let us know somebody was thinking about us. Even if we talked on the phone, something about getting a letter was different. We would even smell the envelope and paper to try to get a whiff of the outside world.

The visits, phone calls, and letters were our lifeline to the free world, but for some inmates, that wasn't enough. Adjusting to prison life isn't easy, and there are no words to describe not being able to connect to the real world. If an inmate didn't receive visitors, letters, or if their family didn't accept the expensive, collect phone calls, they would deal with being locked up in their own way, and some inmates turned to drugs to help them cope from one dark day to another. Drug use in prison wasn't much different from drug use on the streets.

There were plenty of inmates in prison for drug charges, and most of them believed they couldn't live without getting their next hit or high. Medication call was three times a day for inmates who needed prescription medicine. Desperate inmates would use medication call to try to convince the duty nurse that they couldn't sleep or that they felt depressed. They'd tell whatever convincing lie they could come up with to get some pills that might get them high. It might take more than one pill to get high, but they did whatever was necessary.

Inmates who had a hard time coping with living behind bars would ask for pills to just deal with living from day to day. With few questions asked, they were given a prescription drug to basically knock them out, which was only a temporary fix, but they didn't care. They would just go back and ask for more prescription drugs. In no time, the inmate was addicted. We saw this happen a lot. Some inmates would walk around like zombies or sleep as much as they were allowed to. We saw inmates get on antipsychotic medication when they had no visible signs of psychosis.

Sometimes they used the medicine for themselves and sometimes they used it to make money by selling the pills to other inmates looking for a cheap high. A single pill could sell for ten dollars. Manipulation for medicine was a game in prison. Unfortunately, it was a dangerous game, and there were more losers than winners. When the nurse figures out which inmates are abusing the medication, she'll stop prescribing that particular pill altogether, but then that left the inmates who *really* needed the medication without it. This created an environment that was scary as hell for everybody else because we didn't know who was walking around acting crazy or who really needed their medicine because they've been medically diagnosed as "crazy."

Over the counter medications, liquid or pill form, were hot items in prison. Inmates would use anything they could get their hands on to get a high, but getting high wasn't the only reason for asking for medication. Out of pure boredom, inmates played games to see who could take the most pills at one time. For some inmates, life had little value in prison and if they didn't value their own life, they sure didn't value nobody else's life. When the holidays came around, it seemed to only make matters worse. A lot of people that aren't locked up deal with depression even more during the holidays, so imagine being locked up in prison during the holidays.

It took us a minute to get used to spending holidays in prison, and Christmas was always extra hard for us because that was when our family celebrated Daddy's birthday. We thought our first Christmas in the county jail was hard, but our first Christmas in prison was even harder to deal with. Instead of a double celebration, we were serving a double life sentence for eleven dollars – eleven dollars.

Gladys

I'll never forget my first Christmas in prison. I called home cryin' and I felt like breakin' out of prison. I didn't want to escape with a book, I wanted to escape with a bat and beat the hell out of everybody in my way. I woulda done anything to be at home with my family, but instead I was surrounded by a bunch of female convicts who didn't give a damn about me. I didn't act a fool, but I sho' wanted to. I'll never forget that first miserable Christmas in prison. I slept through most of the holidays including my birthdays. I didn't want to be alive, so sleepin' helped pass the time away and helped me forget, for a little while, what day it was.

Jamie

My first Christmas was my hardest holiday. I was in Max, and I remember this six foot Caucasian inmate going to each cell to sing Christmas carols. I cried, and cried, and cried. I felt such an empty feeling inside me, like there was a big hole in my heart that couldn't be filled. The music reminded me of what was taken away from me – my family and my freedom. Besides hearing the Christmas carols, I was also given a box wrapped in pretty Christmas paper and inside the box was different hygiene products. I didn't want to admit it, but at the moment I received the box and unwrapped it, I felt the love of God. I was angry at God, but that small act of kindness softened my heart. I later found out the Christmas presents we were given were donated by different churches. It means a lot when churches or any other organizations reach out to prison inmates – especially during the holidays, when we seemed to miss our family and friends the most.

~

As the months and years dragged by, and as we got to know the other inmates, we eventually started to celebrate the holidays with them – even Christmas. We had a choice. We could either find a way to make the best out of our dark situation behind bars, or let our situation get the best of us. We had a *double life* sentence, so it was in our best interest to deal with it the best we could. We weren't the only ones who didn't want to be in prison for Christmas. No inmate wants to be in prison to begin with, and holidays only made the reality of our life behind bars more difficult to deal with. We weren't alone with our homesick emotions; everyone around us was homesick.

Inmates who had already been locked up for a while knew how to bring in the Christmas cheer in prison, and they helped us. Before long, we were making makeshift Christmas meals with whatever food we could get from the kitchen and decorating the prison walls with handmade ornaments. Nothing will ever replace our family, but we were actually beginning to enjoy the celebration with our new family – convicts.

Gladys

I worked in the prison kitchen, so I would fix a little Christmas meal and give away plates. I did what I could to remember our family's double Christmas Eve celebration. I loved to feed people and was cookin' up some food just like Mama used to do. It didn't taste like Mama's cookin', but my heart was in it like Mama's.

Christmas wasn't the only difficult season to deal with. The summer months were hard, too, but in a different way. The only thing worse than being behind bars in the middle of July was being behind bars in Mississippi in the middle of July with no air conditioning. Instead of celebrating the Independence of our great United States of America with barbeque chicken and ribs, grilled hot dogs and hamburgers, fireworks, and our family, we were celebrating an unjust prison sentence by wiping the sweat that was literally pouring off our bodies. Our cotton uniforms had thick insulation and felt like they were sticking to our skin. There was no ventilation and no moving air to be felt in our big warehouse-looking housing space.

·   No one seemed to care that we were melting – nobody but us and the other inmates who were melting right along with us. Every summer, it was a challenge to not pass out from the Mississippi heat. There were a few air conditioning units working, but they were in the guard towers and in the prison hallways. If cruel and unusual punishment was what the government wanted inmates to experience, they succeeded.

Begging for a fan didn't work, so we sat around with our sweat-soaked uniform pants rolled up and our shirts pulled high while trying to stay appropriately dressed. It was too hot to fight, too hot to argue, too hot to cry, too hot to write the Governor, and definitely too hot to read erotica books, so we tried to sleep the hours and days of extreme heat away and pray that air would miraculously blow our way. We thought the heat would kill us, but it was some news we got that almost killed us.

Our Last Goodbye

A lot can happen in sixteen years – life goes on. Babies are born, and people die. It's a strange feeling to sit in prison month after month, year after year, and get messages about your family members dying off. The longer the prison sentence is, the more bad news we got. Inmates have to pay to attend funerals of their loved ones, and we had quite a few family members to die while we were doing time. We felt so helpless and useless because there was no way we could support our family. On what was already a sad situation, we felt like a burden to our family because they had to pay money before we got approved to go to the funeral service. The family was already grieving and then we make things worse by showing up in orange prison jumpsuits. We felt like we were giving more grief than being a support. It was an awkward situation for everybody.

Jamie

Our big sister, Boonanie, died while we were in prison. She

died from congenial heart failure on July 16, 2008. July 16th is always a bitter-sweet day for me because it's also my birthday. I was able to go to Boonanie's funeral, but Gladys was in trouble *again* for fighting and wasn't allowed to go.

I remember Boonanie's casket being so beautiful. It was a shiny white casket on the outside with white, red, and black on the inside. Boonanie had a Billy Holiday flower in her hair and all the grandchildren and great-grandchildren had one in their hair, too. Shamira, Boonanie's only daughter, was just four years old. I was told that she was in the bed with Boonanie when she died. I walked over to Shamira and introduced myself to her as her Auntie Jamie and she said she knew who I was. It made me feel good that she knew me. I asked her if she wanted to go see her mom with me and she sadly shook her head to say she didn't want to. I didn't blame her because I didn't want to go see my sister in a casket either, but I did.

It was hard saying goodbye to Boonanie, but to be honest, I felt like I said goodbye to her when she got on drugs. Boonanie just wasn't the same. Drugs took her mind and took her away from the family. Years later, we still and always will miss Boonanie's singing and her laughter. We miss our big sister. Boonanie wasn't the only family member whose death we had to deal with. We had cousins to die while we were in prison, and three grandparents. We didn't get to go to all the funerals, but went to as many as we could.

~

One day, we received a message saying the chaplain

needed to speak to us... again. When the Chaplain wants to see you, you know somebody died. Our grandfather was sick, so we assumed it was him. The chaplain brought us together and told us something we thought we'd never hear. It wasn't our sick grandfather like we thought. It was Daddy. The chaplain told us Daddy had a massive heart attack and died. Not Daddy! We heard the words coming out of the chaplain's mouth, but at the same time we didn't – we didn't want to hear. It was like the chaplain's mouth was moving, but no words were coming out. Daddy was supposed to live forever. Daddy was supposed to rescue us out of prison, but instead we were hearing he had died. Daddy left us sitting in prison.

Gladys

I screamed, and hollered, and almost had a nervous breakdown. I lost control. I thought I was gon' lose my mind right at that minute.

Jamie

I started calling Jesus' name. *Jesus, Jesus, Jesus.*

~

Our world was shattered and again we found ourselves in a state of shock. We were allowed to make one phone call – we called Mama. We took turns talking to Mama in the short time we had. We passed the phone back and forth between us and took turns asking Mama questions and crying. We were devastated.

A court order was required to go to Daddy's funeral service. Usually, inmates are only allowed to attend the viewing of the body, but we always requested to attend the funeral service, too – especially this one. After all, it was Daddy. Mama paid for the court order and our transportation to the funeral. We didn't care how much money it was going to cost, and we weren't concerned about being a burden to the family. We were ready and willing to do whatever was necessary to say our last goodbye to Daddy.

Although shackled, handcuffed, and wearing a loud yellow jumpsuit with CONVICT printed on it, three guards escorted us to Daddy's funeral service, which was held in a small, local Mississippi church. The ride was long and quiet. We felt each other's pain and it hurt like nothing we had ever experienced before in our lives. We were going to Daddy's funeral. Daddy was gone. Our protector was gone. That familiar state of shock seemed to hover over our heads and it was hovering lower than usual. We didn't understand what was going on. It seemed like one thing after another was happening to us, and now this.

We got to the church and immediately walked up to the casket and viewed Daddy's body. It was like we had to hurry up and see if he was really dead. We walked together because we were feeding off each other's strength. It seemed like a long walk to the casket. We were both weak and ready to pass out with our hearts beating in unison – heavy and hard.

Jamie

Looking at Daddy, I thought he would get up at any moment. I wanted him to get up. I needed him to get up. I was trying to be strong for Gladys and my mom, but it was hard. Looking down at Daddy, I wondered what we were going to do and how Mama was going to make it by herself with all our children and grandchildren to take care of. Gladys was mentally gone. When we got back to prison, she had to be given shots to help her sleep. I had to be strong for everyone and really didn't get a chance to grieve.

Gladys

I don't really remember how I felt, 'cause I don't think I felt nothing. I felt like Daddy looked – dead.

~

Our only regret about attending any of our family members' funerals was having our kids see us shackled and handcuffed like runaway slaves. Too see us like that shocked them into the reality of their mom being in prison. Saying their mom was in prison was one thing, but actually seeing your mom shackled must've been devastating for our kids. The looks on their faces were like dead stares – blank with no emotion and unable to process what they were seeing.

Embarrassed, angry, and confused only scrapes the surface of what they must've felt. We were also embarrassed, angry, and so sorry they had to see us that way. It was hard for us, but having to leave them to return to prison was even harder. The kids didn't make it any easier when the prison van started to drive off. They would run behind the van until they couldn't run no more. It reminded us of the night we were arrested and taken away in handcuffs in front of our kids.

Jamie

Watching my kids run behind the van broke me down more than seeing Daddy in a casket. Seeing my kids look so lost and confused robbed me of something inside.

Gladys

I was so tired of goin' to funerals. I didn't wanna leave my family and go back to prison. It was so hard, and sometimes I felt like killin' myself. I knew when I got out of prison, if I got out, I wouldn't see some of my family members no more. Daddy's funeral was the hardest.

~

Daddy's funeral was painful for us for obvious reasons, but some of our family members made it even more painful for us by blaming us for Daddy's death. Having a heart attack was the stated cause of death, but his lifestyle, topped with the imprisonment of his young daughters, was the actual cause of death. James Roscoe, our father, died of a contrite, broken heart on February 7, 2003 at the young age of fifty one. Some family members said Daddy wasn't the same after we left for prison, but we weren't the same either.

Daddy's death almost killed us, too. He was our world. Daddy was our backbone and our protector. We always depended on Daddy, but through his death, God showed us that our Daddy was not in control; we had to depend on a Power greater than the man who raised us. Daddy's last chance to rescue us failed. He died and left us sitting in a Mississippi prison getting physically, mentally, and sexually abused. Daddy always tried to keep us from getting hurt, but we were sentenced to a lifetime of hurt, and it didn't seem like there was nothing we could do about it.

Daddy did his best to prepare us to live without him. We felt prepared, but at the same time we didn't. How do you prepare to live without someone who was considered your source of strength, encouragement, and hope? We didn't want to continue living. Daddy was our protection, but it seemed like our protection had been slowly dwindling away since the day they found us guilty. That protection dwindled little by little until it was finally gone, and that was when Daddy was gone.

On the drive back to prison, we felt numb and entered into a world of denial. We knew things would have to change. We knew we would have to change, too. Daddy was the glue that held the family together. Daddy was the one to make sure we had what we needed in prison. He was the family provider. Daddy was supposed to get us out of prison. He was supposed to rescue us, but Daddy was gone.

Days and weeks passed after Daddy's death and we found ourselves calling his house from prison and hoping he would pick up the phone. Reality was setting in: it was true. Daddy was gone and we said our final goodbye. Goodbye, Daddy. Not only did we say goodbye to Daddy, but we said goodbye to getting out of prison. We said goodbye to our freedom. When Daddy died, our hope died. Daddy was our hope for freedom. Our shared life-line was gone, but we grieved in our own way.

Gladys

I started smokin' more, and stayed on the verge of havin' a nervous breakdown. I had to take somethin' to keep me calm. I felt like I was always medicated just to get through my pain.

Jamie

I shut down.

~

Three months after Daddy's death, the system separated

us from each other. We were placed in different units. The prison staff knew we were strong together and they knew Daddy's death took a toll on us. We couldn't understand why they would want to alienate us from each other at a time we needed each other the most. It didn't take long to remember that the prison system doesn't build you up, it breaks you down. We saw family members serve time together in prison and turn on each other, but our love for each other was too strong for that.

They broke us apart physically, but we refused to let them break us mentally. They separated us, but our strong bond as sisters allowed us to feel when the other was hurting or in trouble. We felt each other's pain, although we couldn't see each other. We owe this closeness to Daddy for constantly reminding us to always be there for each other, and to have each other's back. Our sister link will never be broken, and we are so thankful for the closeness we had as little girls, because we needed it more than ever in prison. Our bond wasn't broken, but unfortunately, our will was.

Bodies for Bartering

The worst part of prison for both of us was the continual solicitation of sex from male and female prison guards. We don't want to give all prison guards a bad rap, but the guilty ones know exactly who they are. Any time a female inmate was alone, certain guards would take full advantage of it. Sometimes they even raped inmates – desperate bastards.

Some inmates would agree to the sexual advances just to get something they needed, Other inmates enjoyed the solicitation of sex and looked forward to it. Feeling desired doesn't disappear because a woman is behind bars.

During shower time, the male guards would come to the women's unit to watch us shower. Some inmates liked it while others would cry from humiliation. Writing the warden to complain didn't do any good; they rarely paid any attention to our grievances. As far as they were concerned, we lost our rights when we were processed into the prison system. We lost our name and became a number.

Gladys

Sex is a big part of prison life. It's probably second to cigarettes. Bein' behind bars don't take away sexual desires. Female inmates are still women and some will do whatever they need to do to satisfy their neglected sexual needs. If they had to take it, they took it. When I first got to prison, inmates didn't care that I was pregnant. To them, I was young, fresh meat, and they wanted my body. They didn't know me or know nothin' about me. I coulda had a disease, but they didn't seem to care one bit.

Goin' to prison at nineteen years old made me fear for my life and my unborn baby's life. Older inmates were persistent with their sexual advances towards me and seemed to be experts at manipulation and persuasion. I thought maybe somebody woulda came to my rescue, but nobody did. Nobody wanted to be a sell out in prison 'cause they knew they was gon' have to face some physical repercussions. There was always consequences.

Inmates told me I would eventually give in to the pressure of the sexual advances, and soon have sex with another inmate – a woman. I was told I would never survive double life in prison unless I "got with the system." When I heard this, I wanted to end my life. I was gon' do whatever I had to do to *not* be with a woman. The thought of it made me sick to my stomach. I was afraid of losin' my womanhood, and my mind. When I first saw some of the inmates, they scared me. They looked hard and everybody looked mean. I didn't wanna turn into one of them. I was gon' fight with everything I had for as long as I had to. I wasn't sleepin' with no damn woman.

When one inmate first saw me, she boldly told me I was fresh, pretty meat and that she wanted to sleep with me. *What the hell?* Even though I was pregnant, she kept approachin' me. For a long time, I fought her and some other women off. I was scared to death and nobody helped me – nobody. There was nobody to tell – nobody. Inmates don't have a voice, and the system will always have the last word and win. I saw inmates get beat up, abused, and even take their own lives after complainin' about sexual abuse. I saw female inmates have sex with female guards just to get a bar of soap. Guards took the needs of inmates as a weakness and used it against us to make us weaker. Our bodies was used for trade.

When Daddy passed away, I didn't care about life. Inmates who knew me knew I lost my strength when I lost Daddy. Inmates jumped on my vulnerability as soon as they could and this is when I started to believe I needed to "get with the system." I was tired of fightin', tired of watchin' my back, tired of bein' afraid to go to sleep, and tired of tryin' to survive. I *wanted* to survive. My mind got weaker and weaker. Goin' against everything I believed in and swore I would never do, I did. I "got with the system." I allowed women to abuse my mind and my body. I was convinced I was doin' what I needed to do to stay alive in prison. I believe with all my heart that some of the inmates who took their lives did so because they didn't "get with the system" and couldn't handle the pressure and the physical abuse. This was a real dark time of my life in prison.

The system protects you if you're a part of it. If you're not a part of the system, you're on your own, and you don't want that behind bars. Your identity is stripped from you in prison. I became like the system after many fights tryin' to protect my womanhood. I mean I fought like a dog and I fought a lot, and was sent to maximum security too many times 'cause of it. I broke down – I got weak – I "got with the system." I felt dirty. I felt cheap. I never felt so dirty in my life. I lost respect for myself and for life. Most of all, I felt like I lost my womanhood. I lost me. I felt dead – again.

Sharin' this part of my life brings back a lot of pain and a lot of tears. The pain is deep and it hurts bad – real bad. I feel like I lost a part of myself that I will *never* get back; I will never be the same. When I first got to prison, the warden told me the system would either make me or break me, and he didn't lie. The system broke me – it broke me down. It stripped me from head to toe. I coulda lost my life tryin' to fight off all them women. They knew I would break, but they let me keep fightin'. They was waitin' for me to break like they waited for all the other new inmates to break. Through all my fightin' and all my fears, I never stopped believin' in the power of God, 'cause He was my *only* hope. Daddy was gone, Bigmama was gone, my kids was gone, my hope was gone, and I felt like a part of me was gone. God was my *only* hope. I have to be honest and say that sometimes I even felt like God was gone.

After I had Courtney and had to leave her, it did something to me. I wasn't the same. I felt so empty inside, like I lost my mind, body, and soul 'cause I couldn't be a mother to her. I couldn't nurture her and love her. My natural instincts wanted to, but I couldn't. The anger, depression, and emptiness I felt stayed with me, and it changed me. This anger and emptiness I felt on top of Daddy's death made it easier for me to "get with the system."

Jamie

In prison, we have something called, extra night detail. Guards would get inmates to do petty jobs like pick up trash, or whatever they could find for us to do. I heard some crazy, unbelievable stories about what happens to female inmates when they're called for night detail. Just like most things that happened in prison, I didn't understand why these vicious, abusive acts were allowed to happen, and I made up my mind that I was *not* going to be a victim.

Well, my time came. My first time on night detail, a guard

155

asked me to have sex with him in exchange for some cheap body spray. I couldn't believe he actually thought I would give up my body for some stupid body spray. He sounded like a crazy man and I yelled, *"Hell no!"* He grabbed me, called me a bitch, and told me I was only a convict. He threw me to the ground and kicked me in my side with his hard boots. I fought as long and hard as I could, but he won. He had his way with me. He threatened to put me in lockdown if I said anything to anybody. I couldn't tell Gladys because she would've wanted to fight, and she already stayed in enough trouble trying to keep herself alive and sane. This was just one sexual abuse incident that happened to me. There were more.

Solicitation of sex is heavy in prison and there is nothing nobody can do about it. I got tired of the constant abuse and tried to end my life. I've wanted to end my life before, but this time I was serious. I started getting pills – any pills I could get from the infirmary and saving them. I was *really* hating God around this time. How could a so-called "good" God let something like this happen to me? I wasn't even supposed to *be* in prison and now I'm getting raped?

I saved over forty pills and took all of them. Unfortunately, trying to commit suicide didn't work because the pills only made me real sick. I should've hung myself like Angie did. The nurse probably caught on to what I was doing since I had asked for pills so many times before. The pills I was getting only made me vomit all over the place. I couldn't believe it. After taking all those pills, I was still alive. I was pissed. I guess God wanted me to endure a little more pain, as if I wasn't enduring enough.

Going to prison for something I didn't do, serving a double life sentence for a stupid eleven dollars, and getting raped over and over again wasn't enough for one person to endure? I heard God knows how much you can bear. That's a lie. I didn't want to bear anymore. I just wanted to die. I would go outside on the yards, look up at the sky, and yell at God telling Him I hated Him, and asked why this was happening to me. I may have been physically alive, but I was emotionally, spiritually, and mentally dead.

Being abused turned me into a different person. I started caring less and less about anything and anybody. I didn't even care about myself. The few close friends I had, I started to betray and lie to. I didn't care. I was messed up and confused. I wasn't myself and I felt like I wasn't just serving a double life sentence, but I was also *living* a double life. I found myself being hateful and deceitful, which is not me. I was acting completely out of character. People have no idea what goes on in prison, or in the minds of inmates. The mental state of mind behind the physical and sexual abuse is unreal and beyond repair.

I was also sexually abused by two guards, but to re-visit this in detail would probably mess up my mind more than it already is. For some reason, that abuse by the two guards was more intense than the other sexual abuse incidents I endured. After being released, I couldn't seem to shake the two guards out of my head. I kept seeing their faces, hearing their voices, and replaying the sexual acts in my mind, over and over. I realized I was more messed up over those two guards than I realized. I had a strong desire to confront them, so I did some research and found a way to get in contact with one of them. I found the courage to ask him why he abused me the way he did. He didn't really have an answer, and I don't know what I expected him to say, but he actually apologized and asked me to forgive him. I wanted to believe his apology was sincere. I needed to believe it was sincere, but I know if I was still in prison, he would still be using my body.

Regardless of the circumstances, I accepted his apology and forgave him. I forgave him for me. I needed to move on with my life because my mind was stuck in the years he abused me. His apology didn't take away what he did for six years, but it did something for my spirit…something I can't explain. I stopped feeling like a victim. Do I still think about it? I do, but not as much. The pain will always be there, but it's buried deep and not just hanging out on the surface of my heart and controlling me like it used to. Six years is a long time to be abused, but I know inmates who have been abused even longer and are still being abused. Some inmates are abused for the entire time they're in prison. It's so sad for me to think about the inmates still in prison bartering their bodies and it hurts more to think about the ones having to endure cruel sexual acts against their will.

~

What goes on behind bars stays behind bars, but we want to help change this. We want to be a voice for the incarcerated women *and* men in prison still getting mentally, physically, and sexually abused. Just because we left prison doesn't mean the abuse ended; it still goes on. And it doesn't just happen at the Central Mississippi Correctional Center in Rankin County, Mississippi. It happens in prisons everywhere. The abuse is inhuman treatment and it is criminal. No human being should have to endure what we endured in prison – convict or not.

We know the pain, the sleepless nights, and the shame they feel with absolutely no hope for help. There is no reason to yell or cry out for help because nobody will ever answer. Some people are quick to say those who are incarcerated are getting what they deserve. Trust us, *nobody* deserves what goes on behind the steel walls of prison doors – nobody. If you want to punish someone for a crime they committed, by all means punish them, but don't continually abuse them on every possible level you can think of. That's a crime in itself!

When we first got out of prison, we wanted to keep in contact with some of the friends we made and left behind. We both wrote letters and sent pictures, but all of our mail was returned to us. We called the prison to find out why, and we were told we had to get permission to write. We did our research and found out permission had to come from Mr. Christopher Epps, former Mississippi Corrections Commissioner. We requested permission and our request was denied. We have never heard of this happening to nobody else before. In the entire sixteen years we were in prison, we saw inmates leave and send letters all the time.

We thought maybe our parole status had something to do with it; we're on parole for the rest of our lives. No one has ever given us an answer that makes any sense. We miss the friends we made in prison – convicts. We spent sixteen years of our life with these women. We miss them a lot, and it hurts to not be able to send them a letter. We know, first hand, how a simple, short letter can bring so much joy to an inmate. Some letters are read over and over again for many months, and sometimes years.

Since our release, Mr. Epps, who could have granted us permission to write a simple letter to our friends in prison, has plead guilty to several federal charges and faces prison time himself.

Kidney Failure

Adequate medical care is almost nonexistent in prison. Inmates know not to walk around without shoes and you're out of your mind if you take a shower without shower shoes. We were taught not to touch the walls and we learned quickly to spray and wipe every toilet we sat on. Prison is nasty and it's easy to get sick. We didn't get annual pap smears, mammograms, or even a basic physical. The only time we got examined was if something serious happened to us or if we fell out.

Bleach is only allowed in the kitchen area, so we used a mixture of any cleaning products we could get our hands on to make something strong enough to clean and disinfect our living space like bleach would. We did whatever we could to keep ourselves free of germs, which is impossible, but we still tried to prevent getting sick or catching some disease. There were outbreaks of boils dismissed as spider bites – no joke.

We're not saying spider bites aren't serious, but when you're going to the clinic over and over again for help, you would hope for the right kind of medical treatment.

It wasn't unusual for inmates to find boils on their legs, backs, and behinds. We remember one instance when the nurses were afraid to admit that a recurring report of boils was actually an outbreak of Staphylococcus. The outbreak of Staph was so bad, the inmates infected had to be quarantined in one building. We prayed we wouldn't get sick and die in prison, but it was the diagnosis of a life threatening disease that literally broke the chains off the prison doors for us.

The day we walked into prison, Jamie was overweight and Gladys was a pregnant smoker. We didn't have any health issues that we were being treated for. However, one Saturday evening, Jamie was ordered to go to the infirmary ASAP. It was unusual for an inmate to be called to the infirmity on a weekend since we wouldn't be seen by a doctor until Monday morning.

Jamie

I asked why I was being summoned, but no one could tell me why. It was a long walk for me to the infirmary, and I kept trying to come up with my own conclusion for why I was being called. While I was walking, I remembered having to go to the off grounds hospital to be treated for a gall bladder infection, but I thought it was under control. Because of the gall bladder infection, the system was forced to give me yearly urine examinations, but I hadn't been told that

161

anything was wrong.

The infirmary is located close to where the male prisoners are housed, so female inmates who went to the infirmary had to be placed in a small room behind a steel door with absolutely no air flow at all. I wasn't looking forward to being locked up in a small, stale room all weekend. I was already locked up! I finally got to the infirmary, and was met by one of the nurses on duty. I was given an IV, but still, no one told me what was going on. I asked everybody I saw, but nobody said a word. I felt like they were keeping something from me, so I started to think of the worst case scenario.

I had to stay in the infirmary the entire weekend, and the whole time, male inmates came to the door asking to see my private parts. One guy even had the nerve to ask me for sex. He was obviously desperate to ask for sex from an inmate who was locked up in the infirmary. I found out later that this particular inmate was HIV Positive. Yep, he was desperate – desperate and stupid. Thank God for my self-respect. Monday morning finally came and I couldn't wait to find out what was going on with me.

A short, black man approached me, and introduced himself to me as Dr. Moore. He asked me if I knew the reason for my visit to the Infirmary. Of course I didn't know! He gave me an intense stare and said, "Ms. Scott, you have Stage V Kidney Failure and you need dialysis." I just looked at the doctor with a blank stare, trying to make sure I heard what he said. His words repeated in my head. "Ms. Scott, you have Stage V Kidney Failure and you need dialysis." I didn't believe what I was hearing. I never did drugs, never drank alcohol, or smoked cigarettes, so Dr. Moore's statement didn't make any sense to me. I felt fine. My kidneys couldn't possibly be shutting down.

I selfishly wondered why Gladys' kidneys weren't shutting down. She was the one that smoked and did drugs! I didn't want my sister to have to hear that her kidneys were shutting down either, but why me? The thoughts kept crossing my mind about all the drugs Gladys had in her system and how she smoked while she was pregnant, and was still smoking. *What in the hell was going on?* Out of all the inmates in this prison, why in the world were my kidneys the only ones shutting down? *Damn!*

Dr. Moore explained the unusual amount of protein content that showed up in my urine when I first got to prison that was never treated. The high protein level gradually advanced over the years and destroyed my kidneys. I felt destroyed, too. *My God!* This could have been avoided, so I wondered why no one had said anything to me for so many years. I thought about it for a while, and it didn't take long to realize why I wasn't treated for my high protein levels. It was like a light bulb appeared over my head and started blinking on and off. Why in the world would anyone have any concern for a convict serving a *double life* sentence?

They expected me to die in prison, so why in the world would they care about my health? Why die healthy? It would have been a complete waste of money for the state to treat a convict with a life sentence, and I had a *double life* sentence. As far as they were concerned, I was as good as dead. I wondered why they were bringing it to my attention now? They were either trying to cover themselves, or something else was going on with me that I didn't know about. This definitely wasn't the time to keep secrets – my life was on the line.

Because I had seen so many inmates on dialysis die, my only thought about dialysis was death, so I quickly refused the treatment that Dr. Moore explained to me. Prison is not the place to have dialysis treatment because it's so nasty, so my mind was made up. Not only no, but hell no! The more I sat and thought about the doctor's words to me, the more upset I got. I started yelling and crying and I even cursed God. Again, the question came to mind...*Dear God, what in the hell is going on?* I couldn't understand why God would allow this to happen to me. Wasn't being raped enough? Why in the world are my kidneys shutting down? I cried, and cried. I wondered why it seemed like I was getting punished again, for something I didn't deserve – again.

I secretly begged one of the nurses to sell me some sleeping pills to stop my never-ending nightmare. Of course, she refused. The news I got was just too much for me; I had dealt with enough. My double life sentence, with barely a hint of hope for release, suddenly made a 180 degree turn and became an immediate death sentence with *no* hope in sight. It was true: I was going to die in prison. Just the thought of my devastating, life-threatening diagnosis was too much for me to handle and I fell apart. I cried uncontrollably, like a baby, yelling and screaming and asking God why this was happening to me. I thought I was going to lose my mind. The staff sent for Gladys to help calm me down. Everyone in the prison knew if one of us needed help to go get the other one. Gladys begged me to do what was necessary to save my life and immediately offered to give me one of her kidneys. Life in prison or a life threatening disease wasn't going to break our strong bond as sisters.

Gladys

I had my sister's back. I didn't have to think about givin' her a kidney. My sister needed help and I was willin' and ready to do what I needed to do to help her. I was pissed that she didn't get the care she needed before her kidneys failed, but we didn't have time to be thinkin' about what shoulda happened. My sister's life was on the line. We had to look forward and do what we needed to do to try to save her life. I saw dialysis patients die in prison, too, but this was my sister and we had to do the right thing and follow the doctor's orders. I prayed like I ain't never prayed before. We had to leave prison together, and we had to leave alive.

Jamie

I thanked God for my sister. I didn't want to hear what nobody else had to say except Gladys, and she convinced me to listen to Dr. Moore, and I did. After hearing my options, I was still hesitant, but I agreed to accept the dialysis treatment. Dialysis was given on the prison grounds in a trailer that smelled like it was covered and full of blood. One of the nurses started talking to me about God and I took that as a sign that I would be okay. The nurses made my first dialysis treatment very comfortable for me and I started asking more questions about my treatment. I had a desire to learn more about dialysis, and I also learned the prison's medical motto – *the cheapest way is the best way.*

~

When costs are cut, so is adequate healthcare. And in prison, we barely had *any* healthcare, so a lot of inmates didn't make it out of prison alive. We couldn't believe how sick some inmates got and nobody seemed to really care. The very minimum, if anything at all, was done to help a sick inmate. We watched Staph eat through the bodies of fellow inmates and watched them suffer. We've seen inmates take their last breath and drop dead in front of us. We've seen inmates take medication they didn't need, and the list goes on and on.

Jamie

I had every reason to fear accepting dialysis, but I wondered if the alternative to dialysis would be worse or not. My treatment started in full force, but it wasn't the best. I was in and out of the hospital because I was having complications with the treatment. It felt like my body was rejecting what was supposed to be helping me. I knew I wasn't getting nowhere near the proper foods and nutrition my body needed. I stayed sick. I would get weak, vomit, and sometimes I couldn't control my bladder, so I would pee on myself a lot. I had infected catheters inserted in my neck that caused my

166

veins to collapse, and infection spread through my whole body. I was messed up and felt even more messed up in my mind. I started to doubt if accepting the dialysis was the right decision.

The prison is no place for a dialysis patient because it's dirty, disgusting, and invites infections. Sometimes, I had to be under ceilings that dripped dirty water from sewage and be in closed spaces with molded walls. I had to be on sheets that looked and smelled like they hadn't been washed in months. My fear of dying grew stronger, but I soon found out that what seemed like a death diagnosis would actually be used to literally give me and Gladys our lives back. Mama knew I wasn't getting the proper care I needed; she saw the prison conditions for herself. Mama did what any loving mother would do...she fought for my life.

MAMA

After Daddy died, we didn't worry too much about Mama. We knew she was a strong woman. She was a fighter and there wasn't a doubt in our minds that she would be alright. Mama still blamed Daddy for our imprisonment, and we always wondered if there was some truth to her belief, but for our own father to be the cause for us going to prison didn't settle with us. It couldn't be true.

We know Daddy's death took a toll on Mama, but we were relieved that her fighting days were over. She had been through so much in her thirty-year marriage, and we wondered if she was relieved, too. We knew she loved Daddy, but why all the fights? We remind ourselves of *her* mother, Aunt Gladys, who was such a mean woman. Maybe Mama couldn't help her desire to fight because it was in her blood. Our prison sentence pressed the motherly love out of Mama, and she became more emotionally connected to us, and we loved every bit of it. We were getting some of that love we missed out on as little girls. When we called home, she would end the conversations with, "I love y'all." Hearing those three words meant so much to us, because we didn't hear them from her growing up.

Mama really didn't have a reason to stay in Mississippi after Daddy died, so she decided to move away and get a fresh start. She chose Pensacola, Florida because our oldest brother, Willie, was in the military and stationed there. Before Mama picked up her life and moved, she sold all Daddy's land and possessions and we didn't like that one bit. It seemed like Mama cared more about selling Daddy's belongings than grieving him. We knew that wasn't the case, but it was our aching emotions thinking for us. We were grieving Daddy's death in our own way and we wanted to keep everything that reminded us of him. We knew there wasn't a thing we could do with Daddy's stuff while we were sitting in prison. We had our memories, but we wanted something to hold in our hands, something to look at, and something to feel. Daddy was gone and it was hard to believe he left us in prison. Daddy always assured us that he would take care of us, but the only assurance we had was that he was gone and we were left to take care of ourselves.

Mama needed a change, and we understood that. She needed a new start. Her family had been through what seemed like a living hell, so we were glad to see her make a change for herself. We were already locked up, so it was no sense in Mama being imprisoned in her mind, too. Our family nightmare was more than enough to actually go through it, but to have to be reminded of it every day by your surroundings was like living another nightmare all over again. Although Mama was leaving us in a Mississippi prison, she couldn't wait to get out of the state that caused her family so much heartache and pain. Mama was ready for a new life, and we were ready for her to get the mental breakthrough she desperately needed before she had a mental breakdown.

When Mama moved, we only saw our kids once every six months instead of every two weeks. It was hard on us not being able to see them as often, but we knew they were in good hands. Daddy's death and Mama's move forced us to regroup and find new strength. We had to be stronger. We had no choice. We either had to pull it together and deal with the changes in our lives in prison or settle to be miserable in an even more miserable place for the rest of our lives.

Gladys

We were locked up and Jamie was sick, but we needed to let Mama know we was gonna be okay. We felt like we were lyin' to Mama the way she lied to us after bein' beat up by Daddy. Every mornin' after the fights, she would tell us she was okay. We didn't want Mama to feel locked up right along with us. She had given all of her time and energy to us and raised our kids, so she deserved to feel free. Mama needed to know we supported her decision, plus she needed peace of mind. Knowing Mama, she probably woulda left us whether we supported her decision or not. That's just Mama.

~

We know we have some of Mama's willpower in us. We have a little of her fighting spirit, too. It's amazing how all the pain and challenges we've been through in our lives have made us stronger. We wished we had gone through something else a little less severe and tragic, but instead – and for whatever reason – going to prison for sixteen years showed us just how strong we really are. This entire family nightmare has made us stronger women. We're more aware of what goes on around us. We're more aware of people and their intentions. We're more aware of life. We've become strong like Mama, and God knows our Mama has been through some stuff!

The woman that gave us birth and the woman we witnessed fight for her life throughout her entire marriage started a new fight – a fight for our freedom. After Mama got settled in Florida, she made up her mind to do whatever was necessary to get us released. She knew Daddy wanted to see us out of prison, and it seemed like Daddy's death fueled her new fight for our freedom. In a new state with a new state of mind, Mama put all her energy into proving our innocence. She seemed like a different woman. Mama was a woman on a mission. She started collecting names and addresses for the local media, civil rights organizations, celebrities, and anyone she thought who had a voice to help prove her daughters' innocence. Mama had already lost one daughter, so she wasn't about to lose us, too.

Gladys

I knew Mama was focused, so when she told us what she was doin', I knew she was gon' give it her all. I knew she would do everything in her power to get us out of prison, and she wasn't gon' stop until we were free no matter how long it took. Once Mama has somethin' in her head, she won't take no for an answer, especially when it's somethin' about her kids. Mama was ready to give her life just to give us our life back.

Jamie

When I found out Mama had plans to contact all these people, I went along with her, but I didn't have any faith that these people could help us. Mama was just one person trying to get the world's attention. I didn't want to hurt her feelings, so I just went along with her plan and let her know I supported what she was trying to do. My faith in anything was just about gone.

~

Mama started by writing a letter to Operation PUSH/ Rainbow Coalition, but she didn't receive a response. When we heard she didn't get a response, it deflated the little hope we had, but not getting a response only made Mama refocus and be more determined and persistent to send more letters out. She kept writing to Operation PUSH and added other organizations to her list until she heard from one of them. Mama poured her life into her new fight. Every bit of her time was given to us. She was still taking care of our kids, but her own children became her priority.

After many months passed, Mama finally received a response to one of her heartfelt letters. Ms. Nancy Lockhart, a legal analyst who was working for Operation PUSH, intercepted one of Mama's letters and read it. The letter was actually addressed to someone else in the organization, but we believe it was meant for Ms. Lockhart to read it, and she did. Ms. Lockhart was moved by Mama's passionate plea for help, and called her to hear the entire story about our false arrest and severe and unjust prison sentence. In disbelief of what she was hearing on the other end of the phone, Nancy Lockhart wholeheartedly believed in our innocence, and graciously agreed to help Mama fight for our freedom.

Ms. Lockhart joined the fight and, like Mama, dedicated her time and energy to our case. Knowing a lot more about the Internet and social media than Mama did, Nancy was able to help Mama gain the publicity we needed to bring national awareness to our case. In a very short time, Mama became known across the world as Evelyn Rasco, mother of the Scott Sisters. With her 4'9" frame, big voice, belief in her daughter's innocence, and Ms. Lockhart's guidance, Mama surprisingly reached the ears of listeners across the United States, Germany, the United Kingdom, Africa, and so many other places across the world. Between Ms. Lockhart's passion to explore and expose injustice and Mama's passion to fight for her daughters, a global movement was ignited. Mama said, "Ms. Lockhart was the angel God sent to me."

Ms. Lockhart initiated the increased attention of the unbelievable injustice we were served in our case. Her popular blog, *Free the Scott Sisters*, and her ingenious use of BlogTalkRadio became huge factors in increasing awareness of the "Scott Sisters." Her efforts made a huge impact on social media and caused other BlogTalk hosts to join the fight for our freedom. The numbers of interested listeners quickly increased and the combination of all the support from the different avenues involved created a band of national Internet activists who worked with Ms. Lockhart to get the word out to an even larger arena. The Blogosphere, Afrosphere, talk radio, and so many other media groups caused the Scott Sisters to be of interest to nationally known groups such as the NAACP and ACLU. After sitting in prison for years, two small-town Mississippi sisters *finally* got the attention of nationally known leaders.

After exhausting all of our appeals and not knowing what the next step would be, it turned out that others were prepared to take the next step for us– bold steps. Through the courageous endeavors of Ms. Lockhart and Mama, hundreds of thousands of people that have never met us were fighting for our freedom. These devoted supporters were taking the next step for us through marches, rallies, interviews, demonstrations, postcard campaigns, and any other way possible. These strangers who believed in our innocence and in the justice system were our voices. They not only took the next step, they took many steps.

Radio station owners used their valuable air time and spoke on our behalf, television stations across the country covered our story, newspaper and magazine editors found space in their publications, journalists followed us and reported our story, bloggers blogged, churches prayed, and countless people hearing our story for the first time empathized with us and continued to follow our story.

Jackson, Mississippi supporters even marched to the state capital to ask Governor Haley Barbour to pardon us. These were all bold steps on our behalf. The postcard and letter-writing campaigns spoke volumes of our injustice. We are completely aware that all this was done for us out of love and support from our supports – not one person received payment or personal recognition. Each step that was taken was a step out of pure care and compassion. Nobody had to do a single thing for us, and we are grateful beyond words.

The NAACP, ACLU, grassroots organizations, and Freedom Riders showed up boldly for us. They carried us on their shoulders. When we think of the time, energy, and expertise these groups shared with two simple Mississippi sisters, it's more than overwhelming. It's almost a miraculous act to us, and we can't possibly thank them enough. Everyone made us feel so worthy of the time spent on our behalf and truly validated our existence and innocence while we sat behind bars as convicts. Unless you've been to prison, you have no idea how easily hopelessness and feeling unloved can suppress an inmate. The love and hope we felt from our supporters kept a light of hope burning in us. Our wavering faith was restored and we hoped that one day, we might be rescued and set free from behind the bars. We thought it would be Daddy to rescue us, but another plan was in motion.

There is absolutely no human way possible to thank each person and organization individually; we wish we could. We pray this book will express our deepest appreciation and that the life we now live, although still on parole, will show our gratefulness as we continue to strive to be upstanding citizens in society. Your amazing labor of love to come to our rescue was not in vain, and each step taken was a powerful step that was right on time.

Jamie

My kidney failure, without a doubt, helped spark nationwide media attention. All the uncalled- for, preventable infections, along with the repeated emergency visits to the hospital, put a sense of urgency in all the right places and in the right people. I was wondering if all things really did work together. The word spread about my failing kidneys quicker than the word spread about Sugar Hill. I can't help but wonder what would've happened if my health hadn't failed. What if my health wasn't an issue. We'd probably be still sitting in prison. I shiver at the thought of it.

Once our case started picking up attention, the prison guards kept their distance from us. We were no longer targets for abuse and the guards were literally scared to death to even think about touching us. I couldn't believe it. We couldn't get protection from the inside of prison, but we started getting protection from the outside. The voices of our supporters saved us from another night of our bodies being physically and sexually abused. Our supporters saved us from further verbal and mental abuse. May God bless you all. Sincerely, we thank you more than you'll ever know. Thank you.

It was costing the state of Mississippi close to $200,000 a year for my three-times-a-week dialysis treatment, and it wasn't even adequate treatment. Sometimes the equipment didn't even work right, but with all the heavy pressure from the nationwide media coverage, the prison system had no choice but to give me the proper treatment I desperately needed.

There was no way anyone was going to ignore our cries for help now. As it turns out, the system did, in fact, have a choice and unbelievably decided *not* to continue spending money on my dialysis treatment. Instead, something we thought would never happen happened. In December of 2010, Governor Haley Barbour announced that our double life sentences would be suspended with the condition that Gladys would donate a kidney to me.

Gladys

When I first heard about my release, I peed all over myself. I ain't never did that before – that was Jamie's thing. My body went limp. I didn't feel no part of my body and I didn't feel the stress that always seemed to be built up in me. I didn't feel nothin'. Every muscle in my body was relaxed, and I didn't have no control over it. I was at peace, and for the first time since I entered the prison system, I felt completely calm.

Jamie

When it came over the television that we were going to be released, I couldn't believe my ears. I went and sat on my rack and just rocked back and forth. I cried and rocked, and cried and rocked. I kept asking myself if what I heard was true. I was afraid to believe it and afraid to get excited until I knew for sure it was true. I felt like running, but my legs wouldn't move. I also felt scared because I had been in prison for so long and in many ways, it became my home.

~

We know our release was based on a financial decision for the state of Mississippi, and absolutely nothing to do with the injustice we received. The fact that we were innocent didn't play a part in the Mayor's decision to suspend our sentence. Our freedom was not Governor Barbour's focus, but saving the state money was. The Governor made this publicly clear. He boldly made it known that it was cheaper to let us go rather than to spend money on dialysis treatment. The Mayor's statement of our release validates the prison's medical motto – *the cheapest way is the best way*. The Governor's decision was based on saving money, not saving a life. If you don't believe it, you can read his official statement, below, for yourself. This is also available on the Internet.

GOV. BARBOUR'S STATEMENT REGARDING
RELEASE OF SCOTT SISTERS

"Today, I have issued two orders indefinitely suspending the sentences of Jamie and Gladys Scott. In 1994, a Scott County jury convicted the sisters of armed robbery and imposed two life sentences for the crime. Their convictions and their sentences were affirmed by the Mississippi Court of Appeals

178

in 1996.

"To date, the sisters have served 16 years of their sentences and are eligible for parole in 2014. Jamie Scott requires regular dialysis, and her sister has offered to donate one of her kidneys to her. The Mississippi Department of Corrections believes the sisters no longer pose a threat to society. Their incarceration is no longer necessary for public safety or rehabilitation, and Jamie Scott's medical condition creates a substantial cost to the State of Mississippi.

"The Mississippi Parole Board reviewed the sisters' request for a pardon and recommended that I neither pardon them, nor commute their sentence. At my request, the Parole Board subsequently reviewed whether the sisters should be granted an indefinite suspension of sentence, which is tantamount to parole, and have concurred with my decision to suspend their sentences indefinitely.

"Gladys Scott's release is conditioned on her donating one of her kidneys to her sister, a procedure which should be scheduled with urgency. The release date for Jamie and Gladys Scott is a matter for the Department of Corrections.

"I would like to thank Representative George Flaggs, Senator John Horne, Senator Willie Simmons, and Representative Credell Calhoun for their leadership on this issue. These legislators, along with former Mayor Charles Evers, have been in regular contact with me and my staff while the sisters' petition has been under review."

Gladys

I had volunteered to donate a kidney to Jamie from the jump, so the condition of me donatin' a kidney to her wasn't actually a condition for us, but somethin' one sister would naturally do for another. You don't have to tell us to have one another's back under *any* conditions. I had my sister's back and nobody had to tell me to donate a kidney to help save her life.

~

We had no idea what was in store for us on the other side of the prison walls, but on January 7, 2011, we were released from the place we called home for sixteen years. We were released from a double life prison sentence. We were released from physical, sexual, and mental abuse. We were being released from our family of sixteen years and being reunited with our real family – with our children. The night before our release, inmates and guards were telling us how happy they were for us. We were ready to leave, but as hard as it is to believe, we were also a little sad at the same time.

It's hard to explain being sad about leaving prison, and it probably sounds crazy, but we were leaving our home. It sure wasn't the prison that we were sad about leaving, but it was the sixteen-year relationships we had established with so many women who also called prison their home. We were young girls when we walked into the prison system and were leaving as grown women. Prison was our school of life, and taught us how to be women. We found out who we were and what we were made of in prison, and unfortunately we met the face of justice in prison.

Not everyone in prison was a bad person. We met some kind, loving women in prison. Throughout the years, we laughed with some. We cried with some. We fought some. And we listened to a lot of their stories. Stories of them being raped by family members and physically abused by loved ones. We heard stories from girls as young as sixteen years old having to sell their bodies just to survive. Some women went to prison strung out on drugs and alcohol. There were also some highly educated women in prison.

We heard stories from women from all walks of life. Some stories were so unbelievable that they would keep us awake at night thinking about them. Our childhood stories can't touch some of the stories we heard in those sixteen years. Sometimes after an inmate would share her story with us, we would sit with them without saying a word and shared the silence only another inmate would understand. We met inmates who seemed incapable of committing the crimes they were serving time for. We also met inmates, like us, who didn't deserve to be in prison. They too, were wrongly convicted and sitting in prison hoping someone in the free world would help prove their innocence. We met other "Scott Sisters" in prison. We were leaving them, but we were taking their heartbreaking stories with us. These women shared in the joy of our freedom. We wished we could share our freedom with them.

It was hard leaving our extended family. Some of them have life without parole and they will never see the other side of the prison walls. We were being released, but we knew a part of us would always be in prison. We knew our prison family would continue getting mentally, physically, and sexually abused without any help. Our release was bitter-sweet only because we know their pain continues. There was no sadness leaving the cold-hearted guards – they know who they are. We were finally being released. Just as you might reminiscence about your old stomping ground, when we recall our old stomping ground, it's the Central Mississippi Correctional Center in Rankin County, Mississippi.

From the time we heard about our release, some of our most difficult days in prison started because we *knew* we were going home. We knew we didn't have to be in prison and put up with all the abuse and harsh treatment. It was just a matter of time before we would be free and our attitudes showed it.

Gladys

I started doin' crazy stuff just to get in trouble. I stopped listenin' to the guards and I stopped followin' prison rules. I would walk off by myself, which wasn't allowed, and I even picked fights to try to get in trouble. The guards knew exactly what was goin' on with me, so they didn't send me to Max for what I was doin'. The guards knew I was scared to leave. They had seen it so many times before. I wanted to leave, but I had been in prison for sixteen years – from the young age of nineteen – and I was gettin' ready to enter the free world at age 35. I didn't know if I was gon' make it. It was like I was leavin' home for the first time. I was scared to death.

The morning finally came and it was too much for us to handle. Was it true? Were we dreaming? Had the Governor changed his mind about suspending our release? Our hearts raced when we first arrived on the prison grounds, and they seemed to be racing even faster because we were leaving the prison grounds. It was unreal. It seemed like we were scooped up and processed out real fast, but it really didn't happen like that. It was actually a long process, but it was a blur. It seemed like a dream that we were afraid to wake up from. It was almost too much for us to handle, but we weren't about to complain.

There seemed to be people everywhere around us and there was so much talking going on. Sometimes we didn't know who to focus on or who to listen to – it was just too much. Our hearts and eyes were wide open. We thanked God and everybody else around us. We heard cries, cheers, and outbursts of excitement from a small crowd of people waiting for us outside. It's hard to remember the faces we saw because we were so overwhelmed with so many different emotions. There was so much energy and movement around. Some of the people seemed more excited than we were. The joy they expressed meant so much to us. It felt good to know so many people were genuinely happy for us.

One thing that wasn't a blur was the moment we walked outside the prison. The chains were broken. The place that held us in bondage for sixteen years was releasing us back into the free world. We were free to leave. We were told by other inmates that it was bad luck to look back and, if we did look back, we would have to return. Whether their statement was a myth or a fact, we walked out those prison doors and we did *not* look back. We remember the sun was about to set. It was a beautiful day outside and the sight of the setting sun was like a soothing embrace of peace. Our double life prison sentence was boldly interrupted by a life-changing diagnosis called mercy.

We waited and prayed for sixteen years to be free. We had always imagined running out the prison doors and screaming, "I'm Free!" But that's not how it happened. Our legs wanted to run, but they were so heavy we walked. Our voices wanted to scream, but our overwhelming anxiety silenced our voices. Tears wanted to flow, but we were all cried out. With so many mixed emotions, we can't describe what we were feeling, but we were thanking God for finally answering our sixteen-year prayer. *THANK YOU, JESUS! THANK YOU!*

We were beyond the bars...we were free! On that day, we weren't concerned about our release conditions. We weren't concerned about making it in the free world. We weren't concerned about anything or anybody at that moment besides our freedom! We were free. We couldn't wait to get off the prison grounds to make sure what was happening wasn't just a shared dream, because our release was almost too good to be true. After sixteen years, thirty-two days, and six hours, we were finally free. Inmate #19197 and Inmate #19142 were released from the Central Mississippi Correctional Center. The Scott Sisters were free. Jamie and Gladys Scott were finally free. *Out of the wreck, we rise!*

We were transported from the prison grounds by our

team of lawyers. As we drove off, a sense of indescribable relief came over us. We were *really* leaving the prison. It wasn't a dream after all. It finally hit us: we were free, and it was okay to get excited. The Scott Sisters were free! We rolled the car windows down and together, we hung out the window yelling, waving, and thanking everyone as we drove away from the prison. It was nothing like looking out the window from our fifteenth floor bedroom in the projects. This was a window view we knew we would never forget.

We had to stay in the state of Mississippi for a while and conduct press interviews, which we didn't mind at all. There were so many microphones in front of us and so many people asking questions. Flashing lights from cameras were blinding us, and people were clapping and cheering. It was hard to believe that all the excitement and commotion was over us. We couldn't believe this was all about us. The day before, we were just two Mississippi sisters sitting in prison and the next day, it seemed like we were being treated like celebrities. Things changed overnight for us – literally overnight.

Our lawyers stood close-by as reporters and supporters who fought for our freedom got as close to us as they could to see us and listen to what we had to say. It was puzzling to us that for sixteen years we begged to be heard and now somebody was actually interested in what we had to say. When the interviews were all over, we were able to finally catch our breath and focus on actually going home to see our family. We were going home.

We were anxious to get to Pensacola to see Mama and our kids, but at the same time, it was a strange feeling knowing

185

Daddy and Boonanie wouldn't be there to welcome us home. It was a four-hour trip to Pensacola, Florida, but we didn't care how long the trip was...we were going home. It was a quiet trip; we didn't talk much. We looked out the window and looked at the scenery that we hadn't seen in sixteen years. It's funny how a tree can appear so vivid and green when you're happy and at peace, but when you're in bondage and unhappy, that same tree isn't even noticed. We noticed *every* tree.

We had a million and one thoughts racing through our heads on the drive to Pensacola, but we didn't share any of them with each other. We knew what the other was thinking, so we both enjoyed the peace and quiet and just looked out the windows. When we drove by the water, it was so calming to us. Dear God, we're free. Thank you, Jesus. Thank you, Mama! We wished we could thank Daddy, too, but there were other thoughts running through our head about Daddy. We know why we went to prison, but it's hard as hell for us to accept, and even harder for us to share. We can blame it on the justice system, and we can blame it on the choices we made. We can think of a few things to blame our incarceration on, but one day while we were in prison, Daddy came to visit us.

Jamie

Deep down inside, I knew Daddy could have kept us out of prison. That's why he couldn't look at us while we were in court. When Daddy let those five years pass without coming to see us, I knew something was wrong. Daddy's conscience kept him from coming to see us. Daddy was consumed with guilt. I was mad as hell. I was more mad at Daddy than I was being in prison.

I felt like somebody stabbed me in my heart and left me to die. The man who protected us and made us play right in front of the house to keep us safe watched us get a guilty verdict for something he knew we didn't do. Daddy's girls were Daddy's girls in prison. I felt more like Daddy's *guilt* than Daddy's girl. He put money before his girls, and although he couldn't live with it, he found a way to deal with it. Daddy chose money over us. Daddy's addiction to money took control and sent us to prison.

Gladys

Daddy told us why our family had been harassed. Daddy told us *everything*. He told us about certain people wantin' a cut of his profits and why he was always beefin' with the Sheriff. He told us about his connections and all the stuff that went down at Sugar Hill that we didn't know nothin' about. From what Daddy was sayin', I got the idea that he coulda kept us out of prison by payin' certain people some money. I was mad as hell, too. I understand Daddy's addiction 'cause I had one, but damn, we was his girls. Even when Daddy was in court with his head down, I remember him wearin' clothes to make it look like he didn't have no money. Daddy had all kinda money and everybody in Forest knew it. We didn't have to go to prison, but Daddy's pride and addiction made the choice for us to spend sixteen years in prison – for what?

~

We will always love our Mom and our Dad. It doesn't matter how they raised us, they will always be the only two people we will ever know as parents. Daddy is gone, and we forgive him for his lifestyle choices that sent us to prison. We choose to remember the good times. We could still be mad as hell and bitter, but that's our Dad and his choices don't take away one bit of love we have for him. We understand the power of forgiveness. We miss Daddy.

We knew Mama was cooking a big meal for us to celebrate our release, and our long-awaited for homecoming. Mama always said cooking calmed her nerves, so we knew she had planned a big spread. Mama won her fight and her daughters were finally coming home. We were anxious and nervous to see our kids. We knew they had to be just as anxious and nervous about their mother coming home – a mother they hardly knew. They were babies when we left them, so the thought of reconnecting with them sixteen years later concerned us. How in the world were we supposed to be a mother to them after all those years? They didn't know us and we didn't know them.

Our first stop on the drive to Florida was at a Waffle House. Our first breakfast in the free world was grits, bacon, eggs, and toast. After eating prison food for sixteen years, we looked forward to eating some real food, but we couldn't enjoy it like we thought we would. Our stomachs were in knots. Everything seemed so sudden and so unreal. We sat

188

there and enjoyed being served and not having to rush to eat. For the first time in a long time, we actually had time to sit and eat a meal without a time limit, but we couldn't even enjoy the meal, and we sure didn't finish it.

After Waffle House, we were taken to Walmart to shop for clothes. Wow, Walmart! What a difference from the canteen in prison. We were so excited, we didn't know what to do, so we walked around Walmart and took pictures around the clothing racks and sale signs. We laugh about this now. We bet Walmart would be happy if all their customers came in as excited as we were that day. We got some stares, but we didn't care. We just kept snapping pictures.

As we got closer to Pensacola, the butterflies in our stomachs were fluttering out of control. The time came to be reunited with our kids. We will never be able to thank or repay Mama for what she did for us. Words, money, or the most expensive gift could never repay her for being the mother she was to us and our children while we were locked up. After raising her own children, Mama turned around and raised ours. None of our kids were babies anymore.

Courtney, released to Mama as a newborn, was sixteen years old! We were greeted by mature faces and hugged by young adult bodies. Little faces were also present, and smiled at us – faces that were new to us...our grandchildren. Yes, our children had children. A lot changed in sixteen years. We went into prison as young adults and came out as grandmothers. We changed, and so did our family. We were released to a whole new life.

Just as we thought, a huge spread was waiting for us. Mama's dining room table was full of our favorite foods that took us back to thoughts of our family Christmas Eve party that we were snatched away from sixteen years ago. We seemed to drop right back in where we left off at, but it was a weird feeling. It felt like we were in a time machine and everything moved forward without us. It was a little sad, and took some time to get used to.

Mama cooked candied yams, fresh turnip greens and mustard greens, her famous cheesy macaroni-and-cheese, buttermilk cornbread, barbequed chicken, pork chops, and a dark-chocolate cake that looked so good, we wanted to dive right into it. Mama was *still* working hard for us. We knew it took her all day to cook for us, but she loves to cook. Everything tasted even better than it looked. Mama was still the best cook ever, but little did we know this would be Mama's last big dinner spread that she would cook for us.

We were released in January 2011 and Mama got sick in November of that same year. It didn't seem fair. Mama had given everything she had to fight for us and found herself having to fight for her own life. The stress of everything she had been through had taken a toll on her health and her petite body. Watching her struggle with her health after all she had been through just didn't seem right.

Mama started having serious problems with her diabetes. She was still smoking and she wasn't eating the right foods. It got to the point where Mama had to have the toes on her left foot amputated. She still didn't do any better with her smoking or eating, so naturally things got worse, and eventually her left leg had to be amputated at the knee. Mama got tired of being cut, and she was tired of being in the hospital, but she had no choice. Being used to moving around on her own, and being busy, Mama started to complain and fuss a lot – more than usual. Being an amputee, her mobility was restricted, so her fussing was her way of dealing with her emotional pain. Mama dealt with it the best way she could.

Because of our parole curfew, we couldn't spend the night in the hospital with Mama. We felt bad because she stuck by us all her life and we couldn't even stay with her overnight. It was hard for us to leave her every night, so we tried to do everything possible for her during the day and let her know we were there for her.

The timing of our release seemed to be perfect. We were out of prison just in time to take care of Mama. We couldn't imagine being behind bars and hearing that one of mama's legs had to be cut off and that she wasn't able to take care of herself. She stood by us all those years, and now *she* needed help standing. It wasn't easy for Mama to be laid up and not be able to move around like she wanted to. There were times she felt like giving up. She had a hard time accepting her leg being gone and most of her days were spent feeling frustrated and helpless.

Mama was hard to handle. Some days she flat-out refused to cooperate with the nurses or follow her doctor's orders. Other days she refused to eat. She would ask us to bring her food we knew she didn't need to be eating. It seemed like Mama had lost her spirit to fight when she lost her leg. She was losing weight *and* hope. At one point, Mama got down to ninety-six pounds. It was depressing for us to see her so frail, frustrated, and unhappy. We felt hopeless watching the woman that fought her entire marriage, and fought for our freedom, appear to have no more fight left in her to fight for her own life. Mama had given us everything she had, and we believed she was just tired of fighting. Mama was just plain tired.

We had an idea of what Mama was feeling. We spent many days and nights in prison feeling hopeless and frustrated. We wanted to be able to walk out of prison, but we couldn't. We know Mama wanted to walk right out of that hospital, but she couldn't. We did our best to be as patient as possible with her, but it was hard with all her fussing. Mama fussed about anything and everything. Sometimes we had to fuss back just to get her to cooperate, but she always won. Mama always wanted her way and being in the hospital with one leg didn't stop her from trying to get it.

We eventually stopped pressuring Mama to eat. We stopped begging her to follow her doctor's orders and to cooperate with the nurses. We just let her be. We prayed and called some of our church family to pray with us. A couple nurses prayed, too. We didn't want to lose Mama because of her stubbornness, so we needed all the prayers we could get.

While we were in prison, we wished and prayed that one day we'd be home to enjoy Mama's Thanksgiving feast. We finally made it home, but our first Thanksgiving feast was without Mama; she was still in the hospital. We knew Mama wanted to cook for us, but instead, we did the cooking. Our meal didn't come close to Mama's, but we were home and we were thankful. Before our meal, we took time to remember our friends in prison and we said a prayer for them.

We also remembered the nasty, rubbery tasting ham and turkey they served in prison for Thanksgiving. Yes, we were thankful to enjoy a fresh, hot turkey. To be honest, we would have been thankful without a turkey! We truly know the meaning of Thanksgiving and food is not it. The Scott Sisters are thankful! We decided to take Thanksgiving to Mama since she was in the hospital, so we packed up the meal and the kids and let Mama enjoy our Thanksgiving meal from her hospital bed.

After Mama's amputation came rehabilitation, which promised a long, hard journey for her. Mama slowly started coming around. Her attitude got better and she was a lot more cooperative. We were relieved to see Mama acting like Mama again. Months after the amputation, we realized that something like losing a limb takes time to get used to. Before Mama was given a chance to accept the idea of being without her leg, her leg was already gone. Mama's entire lifestyle changed. We may have been too hard on Mama, but we didn't understand what was going on in her mind. All we knew is that we wanted our Mama to get better. We wanted her to do what she was told, so she could get well.

Mama didn't know how to deal with losing her leg, and we didn't either. She was probably not only grieving the loss of her leg, but still dealing with Boonanie and Daddy being gone. She had lost a child and her husband. We realized she wasn't fighting the hospital staff just because she wanted to, but because she didn't know how to deal with the emotional and physical trauma of all her losses. Our support was important to Mama's healing. We could write another book on family support. That's one subject we know well, and we credit our parents for instilling that in us.

While Mama was adjusting to her new way of life, we were trying to adjust to Mama. After rehabilitation, she was transitioned to a nursing home and we were able to visit her throughout the day and take her places. She could only be out of the nursing home for a limited amount of hours because she was still under doctor's orders. Mama used every minute of every hour she was given to get out of that nursing home. She wasn't able to drive, so we did all the driving for her. We took her everywhere she needed to go. Some days she just wanted to sit with us at our house.

After a while, Mama was able to move out of the nursing home. She was so happy to finally be free of doctors, nurses, and aids. Being in the hospital gave Mama a little rest from all the drama of raising our children. Mama needed that rest, but she was ready to be on her own. Mama was used to being around family and taking care of children. We can't thank Mama enough for everything she did for us. We would have lost our children to the state if it wasn't for her. To tell the truth, we would have lost our life, sitting in prison, if it wasn't for Mama.

Mama's fight for our freedom fueled a lot of positive things in our family's life. Even when we were thirteen and having babies, she took care of them for us, but now that we're grown and have kids and grandkids of our own, Mama's example showed us exactly what we needed to do. When we got out of prison, we stepped in and did what was necessary to take care of our family the best we could. We thank God for Mama's example. Mama didn't just set an example for us, but her fight for our freedom inspired some of our supporters who watched and listened to her speak on our behalf. Her passion and persistence was an example to so many people. Mama never gave up, and we are so happy she didn't give up fighting for us.

Mama speaking out for our freedom

Mama worked around the clock

Mama had her hands full while we were in Prison

One of the many tables of food that mama prepared for our yearly
Christmas Eve Celebration

Prison Family: Gladys front row, second from right

Daddy

Mama and Daddy

Boonanie, our big sister
that passed away while
we were in prison

Our kids, Jamicce, Olivia, Courtney, Richard,
Terrance and Mama

Last family picture before we left for prison

Mama gave her time, energy and life for us

Boonanie's baby Shamira

ANOTHER LIFE SENTENCE

Freedom ain't always free. To be honest, freedom ain't free at all. We were released from prison, however, there were several conditions placed on our release which restricts us from living a normal life. The one condition most publicized is about the kidney transplant, which is the most serious condition out of all of them. We look at it as an act of love rather than a condition. We are still trying to raise money for the surgery, but it's the other conditions we don't really understand.

We are on parole for the rest of our lives. Yes, for the rest of our lives. Because of our parole status, we each have to pay the State of Florida, where we live, $52 every month. It sounds like we're paying the State of Florida rent, and basically we are. If we could save that $52 dollars a month, it could pay for one of our kid's college education. We're not real good in math, but we can do *this* math. $52 a month for one year is $624. Double that, and it's $1,248 dollars. That's just one year! And we have to pay that amount for how long? And people think we're living off the state of Florida for free? Please! Prayerfully, one day we'll be in a position to actually save that money for ourselves. We're in the same situation again, paying for a crime we didn't commit – literally *paying*.

We also have a curfew while on parole. We have to be in our homes by midnight each night, and we are not allowed to leave our homes in the mornings before six am. The City of Pensacola doesn't have a curfew for teenagers, but there's a curfew for the Scott Sisters. We're also required to meet with our parole officer once a month, and she can drop in on us, without notice, at any time of the day or night. The memories of that dreadful Christmas Eve knock on our door, which put our nightmare in motion, haunts us every time we hear our parole officer's knock. We never know who is on the other side of the door, but the firm, hard knock identifies authority and lets us know it's probably our parole officer, and it usually is. Before we even open the door, we fear hearing that we have to go back to prison for some ridiculous reason. It happened once, God forbid it happens again.

Monthly drug testing is another parole condition placed on our release. There isn't a high good enough to send either one of us back to prison. Our traveling is also restricted by our release conditions. Before we cross the Florida State line, whether for business or pleasure, we have to submit a written request to our parole officer. The request has to include names, phone numbers, and addresses of who we'll be with and the exact location of where we'll be. We'd rather not have these conditions, but it's better than being behind bars, so we don't complain. Yes, we've been released from jail, but we don't feel free. If this is freedom, then freedom ain't free. We're *still* paying for a senseless crime we didn't commit – an $11 armed robbery.

We're often asked if we could have one thing, what would it be. Both of us have the same answer. Our one desire is to be off parole and given a full pardon. This would allow us to live our lives like normal people and not feel like we're being watched every minute of the day. We are two, responsible, grown women and we're doing everything in our power to make it in this world. After serving sixteen years in prison, our goal is to *not* go back to prison. The State of Florida couldn't possibly want that more than we do.

In Governor Barbour's last year in office as governor of Mississippi, he gave either full pardons or clemency to over 200 inmates, which included a few convicted murderers. He signed the pardons before leaving his office, and unfortunately, we didn't make his list. Murderers can be given a full pardon, but we can't? That was a chance for us to be completely released from the system, but we were not considered. We have to admit, we were pissed! We were really hoping to receive a full pardon and be able to finally live a normal life without worrying about a curfew or paying the State of Florida rent, but unfortunately the mayor chose to try to keep us mentally shackled. We knew if murderers could get a pardon, our name would surely make the list. Oh well, injustice continues. It sure is hard to have faith in something that gives you absolutely no reason to have faith in it.

In prison, we met murderers, child abusers, and women who killed their children for no reason, and none of them had as much time in prison as we did. We watched inmates walk out the prison doors way before we did. None of them had a double life sentence. We were sentenced to double life for a crime some would have spent 24 hours in jail for. Who gets double life for $11? Not making the parole list should not have surprised us, but it did. Our hopes were high. Our case was definitely an unusual one and probably the only one like it. The fight our mother started is not over. We will continue to fight for our pardon. Mama told us when we were released that she fought for us to get out and it would be up to us to keep fighting to get a pardon. Once the new Governor of Mississippi was in office, we also petitioned him to pardon us.

Denied, again.

We won't give up. We are not a threat to society nor have we ever been. We have not committed any crime to warrant such punishment for the rest of our lives. We are innocent, yet we are treated like criminals. We live in a society where plenty of people are walking around with their freedom who are more of a threat to society than we ever were or ever will be.

January 7, 2012 was our one year anniversary of being released from the Central Mississippi Correctional Facility. Even though we were still on parole for life, we celebrated. We celebrated our life beyond the prison walls! We decided to do something we hadn't done since our release, so we dressed up and went out for dinner and dancing at a local Pensacola restaurant. We had a good time – just the two of us. There was a live band and we danced and laughed all night. We both had a great time celebrating our freedom. In a surreal state of mind, we celebrated an event we thought would never come true. An unbelievable situation with bizarre circumstances, and a mind-blowing outcome. In a nutshell, that sums up our life.

While we celebrated, we talked about how our celebration would not be possible if it weren't for our supporters. We will never stop being grateful for everyone who marched and rallied for our freedom, and most have never met us. We are beyond gratefulness. While we sat celebrating, again we thought about the time, energy, and boldness of all the civil rights leaders, lawyers, activists, political figures, protestors, bloggers, Facebook friends, radio announcers, newspapers, and everyone else who spoke out in our defense – they were our voice..

We weren't familiar with social networking at all, but thanks to our supporters, it worked for us. We didn't have cell phones or computers when we went to prison, but once we were released, we realized those electronics that were so foreign to us were working for us, too. We eventually had to learn how to use cell phones and computers, which was a challenge, but we did it. We definitely had a lot to celebrate. One year went by quickly and boy, oh boy, was it a full year.

The first year of our release was rough, and it started with our family. Since Daddy's death took Mama away from Mississippi, our kids went with her. Mama was busy working on getting us released from prison, so we understood her infrequent road trips from Florida to Mississippi with a car full of kids. She sent pictures on a regular basis, so we were grateful for that. Our children knew Mama, their *grandmother*, as their Mom. She raised them as if they were her own. Mama was the only mother they knew, so our attempt to establish a mother/child relationship with them wasn't just difficult, but almost impossible. They didn't know us as their Mother, so they weren't listening to our instructions or receiving guidance from us. As a matter of fact, they weren't even *trying* to hear us. The only voice our children acknowledged was Mama's.

Regret, bitterness, and blame mixed with a little remorse is what we had to deal with while trying to get to know our own kids. Between our emotions and our kids' emotions, the family stayed in a state of turmoil. Through our eyes, we clearly saw our young-adult children, but in our hearts, they were the babies we left over sixteen years ago. Our babies grew up and we missed it. We missed birthdays, first days of school, and report cards. We missed playing the Tooth Fairy and Santa Claus. We missed nursing them back to health from sickness. We missed lap time and nap time. We missed our kids. They weren't the only ones who grew up; we grew up, too. We all changed. Every aspect of our family as we knew it had changed.

We were away from our family for sixteen years and had false hope of picking up where we left off. We expected a *little* drama, but reality slapped us dead in the face with the constant arguments we had with Mama and the conflicts we had with the kids. We told Mama we had more peace in prison! Our first day back home was like our first day in prison – it was a living hell. We were as confused as we were the few days we sat in court not really knowing what was going on, but trying our best to understand and participate. We were like fish out of water, struggling to fit in the real world with our own family, with our own kids.

We didn't like the way our kids were talking to Mama. If we had talked to Mama that way when we were kids, we would've been picking ourselves up off the floor. Mama didn't tolerate disrespect, but it seemed like her level of tolerance had raised a lot! The kids were taking advantage of their grandmother's love and patience. On the other hand, Mama was probably tired of raising kids and tired of talking. We don't blame her for being tired. She had every right to be past the point of fatigue and frustration. Mama was fighting for our freedom *and* raisin' our children, so she had more than enough to carry on her narrow shoulders. It was obvious that something on Mama's plate would suffer, and unfortunately it was our kids.

We quickly realized it would be a long, hard process to establish any type of lasting relationship with our kids since we were practically strangers to them. Our relationships remain strained and we're taking it one day at a time. There was a time we couldn't sit in the same room together without arguing, and now we can at least speak civil to one another. We get together occasionally for different occasions, and we're getting to know one another, but there is a lot that needs to be said that hasn't been said. And there has been a lot said that probably shouldn't have been said. We were doing what we knew to do, which was trying to get to know our kids.

None of us knew how to properly communicate what we were feeling. There was always a lot of yelling going on. We were yelled at for sixteen years, so that was our form of communication. When we were released, the yelling was released right along with us; it came home with us. Yelling and talking loud is a part of who we are because it's a part of prison life.

We have sixteen years of bad habits to try to break. Transitioning to family life was rough – really rough. Mama didn't understand why certain things she said set us off and we didn't understand *anything* that was going on. We were thrown into a family environment after sixteen years of living with over a hundred female inmates in an abusive environment.

Being imprisoned affected our children more than we realized. Their academics suffered to the point that it just didn't happen. It's sad to say, but only one of our kids graduated from high school. The rest all dropped out – every one of them. They sat in school and endured the comments and stares of other children for so many years. Questions continually were asked of them like, "Where is your mama?" "Why do you stay with your grandma?" "What did your mom do?" "When does she get out of prison?" They also had to deal with their parents never being a part of PTA meetings, parent/teacher conferences, or even having their own mother to sign papers or to be involved in their school life at all. We don't even want to think about the names they were called.

We're sure it would be hard for any young child to focus or study knowing they were the topic of conversation and the butt of all jokes for something they had no control over. There are plenty children of inmates that finish school; we're not blaming their dropping out on our incarceration. We're blaming it on the lack of support they had. They didn't have nobody to talk to or to keep them encouraged. Mama's hands were full, she couldn't do everything. Our children didn't just drop out of school, they basically dropped out of life.

Jamie

Richard, who was ten months old when I left for prison, graduated in 2013 from Pine Forest High School in Pensacola, Florida. I was so proud of Richard, and I was so grateful to be home to watch him walk across the stage. Gladys went to the graduation with me; it was a proud moment for both of us. As I sat at the graduation, I couldn't help but think back to when I dropped out of high school my senior year, and Gladys was a copycat and dropped out in the tenth grade. This was during the Sugar Hill days, when Daddy was preoccupied with making money.

I got my GED in prison, and Gladys later got hers after being released, but I pray Richard is the end of the chain of drop-outs in our family. Richard is now enrolled in Pensacola State College to get his HVAC certification. There are no words to express how happy I feel knowing Richard is moving forward with his education. I too, am enrolled in Pensacola State College to further my education. If I want to see a change in my family I know I have to start by being the change. I refuse to allow the injustice I received control the legacy of my family.

Gladys

When I got pregnant at thirteen years old, Bigmama made me promise to get my diploma. When Bigmama died, somethin' in my spirit wouldn't let me rest until I kept my promise to her. My promise is what gave me the drive to get my GED. I didn't get my GED while I was in prison. I guess I was too busy fightin' and tryin' to survive. But about a year after I was released, I enrolled in Pensacola State College and started takin' classes. The whole time I was enrolled, I thought about my Bigmama. If it wasn't for her, I probably woulda never got my GED. I really did it for her. It wasn't easy, but I did it. The day I went to my mailbox and saw the envelope with my GED inside was a day I felt so excited. I felt like I could do anything that day. I was so proud of myself. I opened the envelope, held my GED tightly in my hand, held it up to the sky, and cried out, *"I did it, Bigmama. I did it!"*

Words can't describe the sense of achievement I felt at that moment. After being degraded and put down for so many years by the prison system, gettin' my GED let me know I could succeed. I knew at that moment that I could make it. I knew everything was gon' to be alright. Yes, I will make it! Getting my GED made me want to continue my education. Whether society will accept my formal education or not, one day, I wanna go back to school – for me. Thank you, Bigmama.

~

Sexual abuse was also something our children dealt with while we were locked up. One of our daughters was raped at a very young age while trying to fill the void of her 'missing in action' mother. She was looking for love and comfort in places where love or comfort would never be found. She has a child as a result of the rape and her own child is a daily reminder of the tragedy she experienced, and it's hard for her to bond with her own child. While we were in prison being sexually abused and raped, we had no idea on of our daughters was also being victimized. We received a letter from her while we were in prison, and she told us everything that was happening to her. We felt hopeless and hurt not being able to be there for her.

We will always maintain our innocence in the crime we were accused of, but one thing we are without a doubt guilty of is that we were *not* there for our kids. Regardless of the circumstances, we were not there for them. A few of our kids were quick to throw in our faces that we didn't raise them and that we weren't there for them when they needed us. It hurt to hear this from our own kids, but it was true...we didn't raise them, and we weren't there for them.

It's a shame we weren't able to instill in our children what our parents instilled in us about being there for each other. If we had taught our children like we were taught, they would have at least had each other to lean on while we were locked up. They could've encouraged each other, but instead they were forced to live as an inmate's child with no support – they were alone. As mothers, the importance of family would've been lesson number one to teach our kids. But we, the teachers, were absent from class. The damage is done and there is nothing we can do about it except move forward. Counseling may give us some temporary relief and help us cope with our life, but nothing will repair the emotional and mental damage our kids have suffered for sixteen years and continue to bear. We simply must pick up the pieces and press on. We weren't the only ones cheated out of sixteen years, the kids were, too. They are trying to regroup and restore what was lost just as we are. Restoring what was lost may be impossible, but starting over was a good place for us to begin.

Gladys

My daughter, Olivia, who was six years old when I left for prison, ran away from home, and got pregnant at age thirteen just like I did. I pray to God that I haven't started a vicious cycle that can't be stopped. I can't say Olivia wouldn't've got pregnant if I had been there for her because Mama was right there in the home with me and Jamie when we got pregnant at thirteen years old.

~

We're trying to connect with each of our kids individually. Each one of them requires something different from us. We're trying to be there for them as much as they'll let us to be. We can only do our part and pray. The adversity we face with our kids feels like another life sentence. This shouldn't be happening at all, but it is. We shouldn't have to go through this and neither should our children, but we are, and we're doing it for a crime we did *not* commit.

Shamira is the daughter of our oldest sister, Boonanie, who passed away while we were in prison. Mama had full custody of Shamira, but signed papers to release custody to us while she was in the hospital. Shamira was eight and not accepting custody of her was not an option for us. Sharmira is a special child because doctor's said Boonanie would never be able to have children. Boonanie was raped by a family member when she was five years old and her genitals were severely damaged. Boonanie gave birth to Shamira, but as a result, Boonanie started having complications and her health started to deteriorate.

While we were in prison, Boonanie called us from the hospital, and asked us to take care of Shamira if anything should happen to her. Even with a double life sentence, we promised our sister that we would take care of her daughter, Shamira. Boonanie must have had faith that we would one day be free to even think about calling us while we were behind bars with a question like that. That phone call we received from our big sister was our last conversation we had with her before she died. To us, Shamira is a living symbol of supernatural power. Boonanie wasn't even supposed to be able to give birth to her, and the fact that we were able to keep the promise we made to our big sister while we were behind bars is more of that same power. We thought taking care of Shamira would be a good thing, and it was. However, our care for our niece caused some conflict with our own kids.

Shamira, nicknamed YaYa by Mama, is young and our hope is to save her from the consequences of growing up without a mother like our kids did. We saw what our prison sentence did to our kids, and it hurts to watch them struggle with their own lives, so we are trying to save Shamira from unnecessary hardship. In more ways than one, Shamira was a huge challenge for us in the beginning. She was already struggling in school with grades and behavior. We know this was because she was allowed to get away with a lot, and didn't get the discipline she needed.

When Mama released custody to us, we went straight to her school for a conference. We were told that Shamira never turns her homework in and was just showing up for school and not really performing like she should. Nobody was making sure Shamira got her homework, which caused her to be working well below her grade-level. We tried our best to help our niece, but we knew we weren't the ones to get her on track, so we found the help she needed and enrolled her in an after-school care program. We know it will take time, but at least Shamira is now going in the right direction. We promised we'd take care of her and we will.

Shamira thinks she's grown, which isn't surprising because she's been around grown folks all her life. She's seen and heard some things she shouldn't have, and we hope and pray it's not too late to save her. Shamira was a challenge for us, and we had to quickly learn patience with her. We yelled a lot, which we knew had to stop. Shamira was a young, innocent child being raised by two women straight out of prison and needing some survival skills themselves. Just like everything else, we're taking it one day at a time. Shamira looks just like her mama, and she's a daily reminder of the promise we made to Boonanie. Shamira gives us a reason to strive for better jobs, more education, and a better life for ourselves. If we have anything to do with it, Shamira *will* finish high school and go to college.

Jamie

We both took care of Shamira when we were first released,

and took care of her like she was our own, but on October 23, 2014, I was awarded full custody of my niece, Shamira.

~

There is a lot of unspoken resentment from our children about our relationship with Shamira; we know this. Our children should have gotten from us what they see us giving Shamira – time. Instead of giving them time, we were *serving* time. Shamira doesn't have a mother or father in her life. We *have* to be there for Shamira. We promised. Shamira not only needed us, we needed her. We swear she's been here before by some of the stuff that comes out of her mouth. We're learning patience and love *from* Shamira, which we definitely didn't learn in prison. We would love to have this kind of relationship with our own kids, but it's not happening, not yet. Sometimes it seems like it's too late for the older kids, but we won't stop trying. We won't lose hope.

We were young mothers in prison, but met plenty other mothers in prison dealing with the same situation; we weren't a special case. Incarcerated mothers can only hope and pray for the best for their kids while they try to mother from behind bars. The prayer of an incarcerated mother is for her kids to remember her. As the family visits, letters and phone calls become less and less frequent, so do the memories in a child's mind. The younger the child is when the mother leaves, the higher the chances are for the mother to be forgotten. The mothers with life sentences and no parole have little hope. No one wants to be a forgotten mother. Every incarcerated mother wants a visit from her child, to hear her child's voice over the phone, or to get a letter from them. Every mother in prison wants to be able to mother her child, but instead, the State is raising them unless the family is in a position to step in and support them. Incarcerated mothers are haunted every day by thoughts of being mothers who've abandoned or neglected their children.

Now that we are out of prison, we want more than anything to help the mothers in prison any way we can. It's a huge task to take on, but it's the simple things that matter the most to inmates. We want to find an avenue to be able to help support incarcerated mothers with children. We know what they're dealing with. We've been released, but we haven't forgotten.

Our family hasn't been our only challenge since we've been released. Unfortunately, we've had some horrible challenges with men also. My God! The games men play these days are crazier than the games the boys played when we were young teenagers. Before we left for prison, we were getting tricked into playing house and strip poker, now men are trying to strip women of everything they have! Our prison smarts didn't measure up to the manipulating games played by the men we've been meeting. Liars, cheaters, manipulators, and plotting predators are just a few words we have for a few of the men we've met.

Jamie

After being around a bunch of women every day and night

for sixteen years, I found myself alone more than I cared to be. I had a hard time adjusting to my life beyond the bars and being comfortable with just me. I felt lonely a lot. Me and Gladys will always have each other, but the midnight hour creeps up and my thoughts wander for companionship in my small, quiet house.

In prison, I had someone watching over me all the time and I felt the strangest need for that same close watch, but not quite the same. I wanted security, but I wanted someone to watch over me *and* to love me. My loneliness led me to seek the company of men instead of getting to know who I was and enjoying my own company. I got involved with a man who made me think he really cared about me. As much as I would love to reveal his identity and scrutinize his name, I'll call him Mr. Man.

Mr. Man told me everything a woman would want to hear from a man. His sweet words made me fall in love with him. I truly thought he was "the one." I met Mr. Man in prison. He worked on the prison grounds, which meant he was well-aware of all the abuse I dealt with while I was there. Surely, he wouldn't want me to suffer any more, right? Wrong. Mr. Man didn't care about me at all and played the player's game. He lied to me and used me. I found out too late that I wasn't the only one he was lying to and using, and my love for him was already too far gone to reel back in. I was one of many women falling for the same man.

He took advantage of my vulnerability and my obvious need to be loved. I knew I needed to let this man go, but it was so hard. It wasn't just hard, I didn't *want* to let him go. I stayed with him hoping he would change and hoping his next, "I'm sorry," was his last one. The change I hoped for never came and he only treated me worse. I learned the hard way that a man will do whatever a woman lets him do. I let Mr. Man play with my feelings. I knew I needed to walk away, but I chose to stay. Somehow, Mr. Man managed to make me feel like I was the one treating *him* wrong. When I threatened to leave him, he would make me feel guilty. I finally got tired of feeling like a fool and found the strength and courage to love myself enough to boldly walk away.

It took time to shake Mr. Man out of my mind, and I even went back to him a few times before my foolish tank ran over. It was a struggle, fighting the thoughts of him creeping into my mind. I thought Mr. Man was interested in me, Jamie Scott, but instead he was only interested in satisfying his physical needs. I was just another female he used to release his out-of-control sexual cravings. Bastard. I was devastated and heart-broken. I felt like a dummy for falling for no-good Mr. Man, and a bigger dummy for going back to him over and over. I was hesitant of getting into another relationship, but my cautiousness worked in my favor because my focus is now falling in love with my God and taking care of myself. I'm learning to enjoy my own company and not have to have a man to feel loved. Some men are just like the Devil. They come to kill, steal, and destroy.

I pray I won't fall for the lies again. I know there are still some good men in this world, but before one crosses my path, I have to live as a Godly, single women. I knew giving my body to Mr. Man was wrong, but I allowed my own desires to speak

219

and lead me right into his arms of deceit. I should have listened to my brain, but my heart beats were louder. If I'm good enough to share a man's bed, I should be good enough to share his last name. I'm learning to love myself a little more every day. Is it easy? No! It's not easy being a single woman. I think all women want a nice man in their life to spend time with, but it's not worth our time or self-respect to be with someone who only wants to give us bedroom time. One day I would love to meet the *right* Mr. Man – a man who will truly love and accept Jamie Scott. Sixteen years of my life was spent in prison, I refuse to be imprisoned again by another man's trifling games and selfish ways.

~

Another challenge we continue to face since our release is a term used a lot in prison – the "general population." We were warmly welcomed in Pensacola, Florida, but there are always a few bad apples and we've met our share. It took a minute, but we found out that everyone who wanted to help us didn't always have our best interest at heart. At first, it was hard for us to believe "sincere" helpers had an underlying motive, an agenda of their own. We were reminded of how cautious we were of other inmates when we first got to prison. We knew we couldn't trust anyone and we were leery of the ones who wanted to get too close too soon. We are still cautious today. Both of us have some serious trust issues.

Some people see only dollar signs when they see us. We

thought only the wealthy had this problem, but we proved that to be a lie. We're rich in strength, faith, and hope. We wish we could see all those dollar signs other people see on us. The Mississippi Department of Corrections sent us home with a $75 check. We live from paycheck to paycheck, and we're always helping each other when one has more month than money. Some people actually believe we are rolling in dough, which is ridiculous. We are far from rich, but people are sticking close to us like they're waiting for some big payoff.

Because of the large amount of media coverage we had, a lot of people looked at us like celebrities when we were released. Some assumed we would automatically come out of prison like two wealthy women with movie deals and book offers, plus requests to appear on national television talk shows. The only deals and offers we had were for jobs! We struggled when we got out of prison. There was no movie deal waiting on us, and the paparazzi sure wasn't following us. The only thing that followed us was the felony record that kept reminding us of our sixteen-year prison sentence for eleven dollars that we knew nothing about. We were thrown into the struggling economy and had to find work just like the next person.

~

Attorney Lumumba Chokwe, the NAACP, and other organizations joined together to help us with our transition from prison. We dare not mention individual names to thank the people who helped us settle in Pensacola. One person's prayer for us was just as appreciated and important to us as the help we got with housing and employment. A simple smile and accepting us for who we are in spite of our past meant the world to us as we got adjusted to our new community. We can't change our past, but we're doing our best to make a better future for our ourselves and our kids.

Words can't express just how rough our first year out of prison was, but we made it through. Getting adjusted in a society that progressed sixteen years while we stood still, took more than a minute to get used to. We were scared out of our minds the first few months after we were released and we had to quickly change our way of thinking. For sixteen years, we were told when to wake up, when to walk, when to eat, when to sleep, when to shower, and how to do it. After being released from that structured system, we realized that if we didn't get out of bed every morning, nobody was going to care. If we didn't find a job, nobody would care. We weren't waiting for something to happen anymore; we had to *make* things happen. We had to find the initiative to make a life for ourselves.

"Instead of making excuses, find a way to make things happen."

Robert Hill, WRNE 980 AM / Choice 106.9 FM

Pensacola, FL

In prison, our life was made for us. Life was mapped out by the minute and every day was planned. We didn't have to think for ourselves in prison, so when things happened in the real world, we had to learn to think for ourselves. It was so easy to pick up the phone and ask for help, but people weren't always available to us like we wanted them to be. Everyone else was trying to live their own lives with their own issues, so we had to learn to live ours, too. It was rough.

Most days we felt lost and without direction. Everybody was going on with their lives, but we were trying to find ours. We almost felt like we needed to hold somebody's hand through our transition to the free world, but we were grown women, so we had to make things happen the best we could. We didn't stop calling folks when we needed help, but we knew not to call as often as we did when we were first released. We wore a few people out with our phone calls, tantrums, and self-proclaimed emergencies, and they know who they are. We love you! They didn't judge us or ask us to stop calling, but they understood our calls were calls for help – literally. There were a lot of things in the free world we didn't understand, and a lot of people we didn't understand.

We were basically forced to be productive citizens with no formal training or preparation besides the home-training we got from our parents as kids. We were nineteen and twenty-one when we left for prison. It wasn't easy for us to adjust to life beyond the bars.

Jamie

I was having such a hard time adjusting to being in the free world that I actually thought about going *back* to prison. Life was easier in prison because I didn't have to think for myself. I didn't have to learn to get along with folks because we just argued and fought in prison. I didn't have to pay bills in prison or be concerned where money was coming from. Daddy always made sure money was in my prison account. In prison I felt like I was fighting for my life, but in the free world, I was struggling to *live* my life. I was physically and mentally drained of all efforts to fight and struggle for anything. I was tired.

~

We probably moved way too fast when we were released by getting our own places and having our own cars without any money management training. We were thankful for those who helped us get settled, and we were ecstatic to have a place to live and a car to drive, but the bills and maintenance to maintain those things trickled in fast and caught us off guard. The trickling was more like a flash flood to us because there were no bills to pay in prison. In prison, all we did was wait for Daddy to send us money – and we spent every penny of it. We were forced to learn to budget the little we had. We juggled our spare change to keep our lights on and keep gas in our cars. We had to eat out less to save money for unexpected expenses like repairs on our cars. Those expenses popped up out of nowhere! When gas prices started to rise, so did our eyebrows. Even with jobs, sometimes we had to borrow money because we were barely making it.

We were learning to live all over again, and we were learning to live with Shamira, our niece we had custody of. We couldn't just think of ourselves, we had a child to think about, too. We had to work around her school hours and after-school tutoring. We had to make sure she was picked up on time and in bed on time. This was normal everyday life for society, but it wasn't normal to us. We felt like we were trying to catch up with life, and always being a step behind.

Gladys

We had so much goin' on. Jamie had to work 'round goin' to dialysis and the gym, so she could lose weight for her kidney transplant. We had our mother to help take care of and our kids to deal with. A lot of things went into the jobs we chose, so we moved from job to job a lot of times until we found the right pay, the right schedule, the right distance to save gas, and the right employers who understood we was tryin' to survive mentally, socially, emotionally, and financially. It just wasn't easy. As a matter of fact, it was hard as hell. If we didn't find good payin' jobs, we couldn't pay our rent, which meant we woulda been homeless, which meant findin' a job woulda been out of the question. There was pressure every day from every direction just to survive.

~

Every day we have to encourage ourselves. 2011 was our bumpy transition year, and 2012 was our year of tests and trials. Each year got a little easier. Everything and everyone has been a learning experience for us to build on. If we met

225

you, we learned *something* from you.

We have to be careful about the moves we make. One wrong move and we're back in prison. As unfortunate as it is, being on parole for life makes us an easy target for the law. A random stop by police officers has the potential to land us right back in prison. Being accused of not having a valid driver's license or car insurance, when we clearly have proof of both in our possession, could be devastating for us. Unfortunately, it has happened.

Jamie

On my way to church one Sunday morning, I was stopped by a Pensacola police officer for a supposedly "random" stop. The "random" Sunday morning stop left me standing on the side of the road without transportation. Let's just say, I'm glad I didn't wait to get to church to have church. I was already prayed up. I didn't have a problem when the officer questioned me and asked for my paperwork. I didn't get upset until he told me my insurance had expired, which wasn't true. I was so angry. The words I thought about saying could have easily landed me back in prison. I was already praying and praising God before I got stopped, so I was able to maintain my composure and be as respectful to the officer as I could be under the "random" circumstances.

When the officer told me I wouldn't be able to drive my car, I prayed about how I was going to get home. This "random" stop was the most unusual stop I had ever experienced. Within minutes, I saw Gladys driving by.

Coincidence? If you believe it was a coincidence for my sister to just happen to drive by while I was standing on the side of the road on a "random" Sunday morning, then you also believe it was a coincidence for one of the "Scott Sisters" to be pulled over that morning for a "random" check and left stranded.

. These types of situations scare the hell out of us, and make us feel like our nightmare is rewinding and playing all over again. When we come in contact with these bad apples, we simply have to throw them out and keep going. We know there are more bad apples to meet, so we try our best to use them to strengthen us for the next rotten bite. It isn't easy, but this is our life, so we're learning to live it. Injustice? There's got to be a another word for what we've been through and are still going through. The word "injustice" just doesn't seem strong enough.

We know our convictions are following us, but is Mississippi justice following us, too? Have mercy! This is crazy! Will we ever be able to live a normal life? Is being on parole for life not enough? If we moved to Iowa or Ohio, would we be free from false accusations? We'd like to think so, but they probably have "random" stops in those states, too. We know everything happens for a reason, and even that "random" stop was a lesson for us. We learned something from it. Those sixteen years behind bars were jam-packed full of lessons. We would've never chosen prison to be our life coach, but for whatever reason, it was. Were we "randomly" chosen to be the Scott Sisters? We don't think so. Our kids weren't "randomly" chosen to be kids of convicts either.

Kids are known to follow in the footsteps of one of their parents. We've made some unwise choices in life and our kids seem to be terrifyingly following in our footsteps. We dropped out of school and so did they. We grew up in the projects and now they're living in the projects. We've been to prison and now...

Jamie

I went back and forth on whether or not to share this part of my life with the world because it hurts so bad. I decided to share because it shows just how much our imprisonment has affected our kids. Mississippi injustice not only touched our life, but it touched our kids' lives. The decisions parents make in life touch *every* member of the family in some way. With us, the cycle seems to be non-stop. My son, Terrance Scott, is more like me than any of my kids. We nicknamed him Moon because his face was round like a full moon when he was born; it was almost a perfect circle. Terrance is in prison now. I asked Moon to share his heart.

Terrance Scott, a/k/a Moon

If I could turn back the hands of time, I would go back to the sixth grade when a boy asked me what side of town I lived on. I told him the East side and he said, "F– the East side." That one simple statement made me mad and I beat him up. I found out later that I broke his jaw and I got suspended for

228

that fight.

How I responded to that boy's response changed my life. If I could do it over again, I would have said, "I'm from planet Earth, where you from?" That one fight led to another fight... that led to another fight...that put me out of my school. I had to go to another school and got put out of that school, too. Alternative school was the only thing left for me. It was alright for a while, but I started fighting there, too. I started skipping classes and then stopped going all together. I missed two months of school without my Grandma knowing. I always planned it just right. I got dressed and had my back pack like I was going to school. The school finally got a hold of Grandma and my fun was over.

I finished the eighth grade and that was it for me with school. I chose to graduate with street smarts instead of book smarts. I didn't go to high school at all. I finished the eighth grade and jumped right in the streets. I saw guys selling drugs and making big money, so that's what I did. Selling drugs brought in a lot of money, but it took my life away. Now, I'm sitting in prison.

I don't have an excuse for getting into trouble. I missed my Mama and I got tired of seeing my Grandma struggle with money and miss meals just so me and my brothers, sisters, and cousins could eat. With Mama and Auntie (Gladys) in prison, my grandmother had a lot on her and she had a lot of kids to take care of. She was always busy doing something.

I started hanging with my "homeboys" and learned how to make money selling drugs. I sold drugs to all kinds of people – rich people, poor people, people from all races and different backgrounds. We knew where to go to sell the drugs and drug users knew where to come to get them. It was crazy. I was real young and got caught up with the wrong people, and was in the wrong places at all the wrong times and ended up in jail. It wasn't just drugs that sent me to jail, because with drugs come guns. I started making all the wrong choices and it all started with that one fight in school.

Those "homeboys" never sent me a dollar while I was in the county jail or came to see me or write me a letter when I was sent to prison. The only time my "homeboys" cared about me was when I was hanging with them in the streets. They had my back then, but I needed them to have my back when I went to jail, but they weren't there. They were "homeboys" as long as I was hanging with them and getting in trouble with them, but when *I* got in trouble, they were nowhere around.

I missed my Mama so much. I had a hard time dealing with her being gone. I felt like a hole was in my heart. I went to see her once a month and remember her wearing either black and white or an orange jumpsuit. The only time I remember her wearing regular clothes is the day the sheriffs came and took her away from me. I see her in regular clothes now when she comes to visit me. To see her in regular clothes and free makes me smile – it makes me so happy to know my Mama and Auntie are free after all those years. I didn't like that they were in prison at all. That was real hard to deal with.

I remember the night the police dragged my Mama away. I

was only two, but I remember trying to run behind the police car to get my Mama. My Grandma pulled me back. I was so young that all I knew was somebody was taking my Mama away. That was my Mama! I was traumatized that day, and will never *ever* forget it. I remember crying hard for Mama – I couldn't cry hard enough. I thought maybe if I cried long and hard enough, somebody would see my pain and bring her back to me.

As I got older, the pain didn't stop – it just grew stronger and stronger. I remember being in the sixth grade and getting in trouble because I missed my Mama so much. I guess I was trying to express my pain. I didn't understand what was going on. I didn't care about nothing except my Mama coming home. I will *never* forget the night the sheriffs dragged my Mama away from me. It plays back in my mind over and over. It hurts.

Mama was gone for sixteen years, so I had to get to know her all over again. I was young when she left and you can't get to know somebody in prison by visiting them only a few times a year. I wanted to know what her hobbies were and what she liked doing in her free time. I wanted to know what her favorite color was. I knew my Mama, but I didn't know my Mama. I wanted to know who my Mama was and everything about her.

Prison stole my Mama. I don't even feel like she is the Mama that left me because I know prison changed her. After sixteen years, it *had* to change her. All I know is that my Mama is free and I love her so much. It's a wild feeling when Mama comes to visit me behind bars. I used to go visit her and now she's visiting me. It blows my mind how the table turned. We switched places, but I'd rather be behind bars rather than have my Mama behind bars. I can't tell you how happy I am that my Mama is free. That's my *Mama.*

Everything my Grandma told me came true. She would always tell me I was going to end up in prison if I didn't slow down. She always reminded me of the men in our family who went to prison. I regret everything I did, but in 2003 when my grandfather, James Rasco, died, I really lost it. First Mama left me, and then Grandpa. I didn't know Grandpa was dealing with drugs until his funeral. The word got out that he was drug dealing, and everybody was talking about it. I remember Grandpa being a gentleman and I never would've believed he was a drug dealer. It's good children don't see grown folks for who they really are. My grandfather was the only positive male influence I had in my life. I had my Grandma, but a boy needs some type of male figure in his life to keep them on the right path; I know I did. Grandma was always busy doing something and she had a lot of kids to take care of. It was a lot of us and just one of her.

If I could tell young kids one thing from behind these bars, I would tell them it ain't worth it. Whatever they're dealing with in the streets, it ain't worth it. I want to write a book about the mistakes I made in life to help other people making bad choices. If I can help somebody else, I will. I regret everything I did.

Jamie

When I visit Moon and talk to him behind that glass, it takes me back to my days of being locked up. It's a strange feeling – almost eerie. When I hear the doors lock behind me, something goes through me and my first thought is always if I'll be able to get out. I pray Terrance will be okay. That's all I can do is pray. Sometimes I feel responsible for him being in prison. I wonder if things would be different for him if I had never gone to prison.

I wanted Moon to be a part of this book because it shows to what extent injustice touched our kids. No, I'm not blaming the system on Moon going to jail, I'm putting the spotlight on the justice system and how convicting innocent citizens can take a toll on so many other lives. Injustice changed our entire family. All of our kids have a story to tell – heart wrenching stories. Each of them could write their own book and share what they went through as a result of our incarceration. It's a sad situation all around, but it's their life – it's our life. We don't have a choice except to look forward. Looking back will only hold us back. We didn't think we would make it this far and a lot of people didn't expect us to make it at all, but God!

We love each other

We don't know what we would do with out one another

Jamie and her children, Richard and Jamicce

Our grandchildren mean the world to us

Richard and Jamicce

Gladys and her children, Olivia and Courtney

Gladys and her daughter Olivia

Gladys and her grand-daughter Gracie Mae

Gladys and her grand-son Xander

...BUT GOD!

From the first day we entered into the prison system, we prayed and asked God to set us free. If no one else knew we were innocent, God knew, and He still does. Every day of prayer turned into another day in prison. Our prayer went on for sixteen years. There were times we didn't think God heard our prayer and there were other times we didn't think God cared. We wondered if we were being punished for something, or if God was trying to teach us a lesson. If so, our time is prison was one long, hard, sixteen-year lesson.

Jamie

I was so angry, I felt like God owed me something. God interrupted my life and I didn't like it. I didn't ask for none of this. My family was torn apart and to this day, my kids don't really know me.

Gladys

I stayed angry all the time while I was in prison, but I kept hearin' Bigmama in the back of my mind tellin' me to believe in God no matter what happened in my life. Believin' in God was my only hope. I didn't have nothin' else to hold on to or to make me want to keep goin'. Hope kept me goin'.

Did our sixteen-year prayer shake our belief in God? There were days we doubted God, and yes, our belief was shaken, but we never stopped believing in Him. How in the world could we stop *believing* in God? We learned from Bigmama that God wasn't a God of convenience, but a God of conviction – a God of change. Sure, we wanted God to be a magician and wave His holy, magic wand over the Central Mississippi Correctional Center and let the steel doors miraculously open. We wanted God to make the jury find us *not* guilty. Any of those magical acts would have been convenient for us, but none of them happened. At no point did we *ever* understand what was going on with us. None of it ever made any sense to us and to be honest, it still doesn't make any sense to us.

If we understood God, we wouldn't need God. We're asked all the time, how we managed to survive being falsely accused and still living on parole. We just have to live from day to day the best way we know how, and that's to wake up every day with hope to get through the day – it's as simple as that, because we don't know to do anything else. We have to have hope in something bigger than us. Everybody else had let us down or left us. The only thing that was left in our life that we could depend on was hope.

We learned how to take one day at a time in prison. With a double life sentence, we didn't have a future to think about, so we really didn't have a choice *except* to take one day at a time. As inmates, our tomorrows literally took care of themselves. Morning after morning, we woke up confused, angry, and wondering what was going on. Our only hope *was* an almighty God. Nobody *but* God could have broken our shackles and set us free through the voices of hundreds of thousands of people we had never met. There was no way in the world we were about to turn our backs on God. Even when we doubted Him, we still had a flicker of faith. The power of God was planted deep in our minds by Bigmama. We heard about how good her God was way too many times.

We've been asked why we give God credit for our release when it took Him sixteen years to do it. If we were released in six days or six hours, would God deserve the credit? What's the time frame for prayers to be answered in order for God to get the credit? The time frame doesn't matter to us, but the fact that it happened does. We may be on parole for life, but we have life, and we've been released from prison. We *boldly* say God answered our prayers, and He used a lot of vessels in the process to make it happen.

Of course, we would've preferred not to have gone to prison at all, but we did. We wish Daddy would've made better choices in his life, but he didn't. There is nothing we can do about anything. We can either keep rewinding the incidents in our minds, or we can learn from them and move on. It's not our job to convince anyone or to justify God's actions. Our only obligation is to tell *our* story of how God kept us for sixteen years of mental, physical, and sexual abuse and released us when we were supposed to die in prison. We had a *double life* sentence, but God!

We know we're a very small part of a much bigger picture. Pensacola's beautiful beach sand reminds us of just how small our part is in this big world. We look at every grain of sand like it represents someone's life. We're just two small grains of sand wanting the attention of one big God. We believe God is in control of everything we went through and everything still to come. We had faith in prison, but our faith waivered. We questioned God, we doubted God, and even cussed God, but we had nothing or nobody else to hold on to, *but* God. We were so confused, but convinced that nothing else could help us cope but our faith in God. What else

was there? Who else was there?

After being released, so many people started out with us, but left us. Some saw us only as ex-convicts and were afraid to be around us. Some were afraid for us to be around their kids or in their homes. Some thought we were just dead weight and thought they were wasting their time with us. We understand we have a past, but we had to depend on someone who didn't care about our past, but was concerned about our future. We had to depend on someone who promised to never leave us. Like we said before, sometimes we even wondered if God was there for us, but something would not let us walk away from Him.

We are still going through some things, and we know more is to come, but God! To be honest, everybody may not go to prison, but everybody has a past. We hope after reading our story that people aren't so quick to judge us before you get to know us. Since our release, some days are a whole lot harder than others. Anger and resentment from our years spent in prison rise without warning, so we have to constantly remind each other to stay encouraged. We have to

241

The first few weeks after being released from the nasty prison food was a real hard time for me. I was surrounded by a whole world full of good food, I wanted to try everything. It wasn't the most ideal time to try to lose weight. I didn't think I would be able to do it because I felt tempted to eat all the wrong foods all the time. I wanted to taste foods I hadn't eaten in sixteen years, but each taste led to another taste. When Mama cooked that big spread to celebrate our release, I didn't think about losing weight, I just wanted to enjoy the celebration, and all of our family celebrations are surrounded by food. It was a challenge to lose so much weight, but in the back of my mind, I always thought about the alternative to not losing the weight. That helped me get back on course whenever I needed to, which was often in the beginning.

Having the kidney transplant was the main reason we were released, but unless I lost the weight, the transplant wasn't happening. I wasn't about to take a chance with my health or my freedom, so I joined a local gym called Pensacourt. I started going to aerobics five times a week and trying to do better with my food choices, but it was real hard not stopping at fast food places. After sixteen years, fast food places seemed like they were calling my name. It was a struggle, a big struggle, but I finally got on track. I wasn't doing all the right things, but I was doing a whole lot better and I started feeling better, but the weight wasn't coming off.

At first, I felt like I was wasting my time because I had so much weight to lose and wasn't seeing results, but I just kept doing what I knew to do. I kept going to the gym and doing my aerobics and whatever else I knew to do. I had two people who were in my corner and understood what I was going through. Gibson Piccioli and Cory Wooten were the people that really supported me in my weight loss. They were always there for me and pushed me pound by pound until the weight came off. They really cared about my progress, and I'll be forever grateful for their love and support. There is no way I could have done it without them. I didn't have the discipline by myself, but they had the patience. They were awesome.

Eventually, the pounds slowly starting coming off, and some pounds would even come back on. There were days I would feel so discouraged that I would eat, knowing I was hurting myself and prolonging my surgery. But again, I finally got it together. There isn't anything easy about losing weight, but I'm proud to say that I have less than 40 pounds to go before I'm at the weight needed to have my surgery. These last pounds are hard to lose. I can't seem to shake them, but I'm doing what I need to do to stay alive. It took a long time, but I'm getting there.

I've got to keep pressing on. Life is short, and sometimes I feel like my life is even shorter because I was locked out of life for sixteen years. Since I've lost almost all the weight to have my surgery, I found out I have to have another surgery to remove all the loose skin before I have my kidney transplant. *Dear God, what else can happen?* I don't have the money for this surgery. It's difficult to save money period, and now I have to save several thousands of dollars to have this surgery. My heath isn't on the line, my life is on the line. When I first found out about the surgery and how much it costs, I was devastated. I couldn't figure out how I was supposed to come up with that kind of money when I had trouble coming up with money for my bills. Gladys and I thought of several ways to raise money, but we really didn't know how to go about having a fundraiser besides doing what we know, which was cooking. We thought about having a fish fry, but we didn't even have the money to buy the fish! At this point, I'm just trying to save the money the best I can, so I can eventually have my kidney transplant.

~

A lot of people have a defining moment in their life or as Christians call it, a "Damascus Road" experience. Whatever you call it, this defining moment is supposed to trigger change in your life. Our sixteen years in prison were definitely our Damascus Road, and a very long road it was. As a matter of fact, we're still traveling that road. It's a long journey. Our journey, for the rest of our life, will be a serious attempt to seize every moment instead of thinking about what should've or could've been. We can't recapture lost years. We tried for a year and it didn't work. Those sixteen years are gone and we are not promised sixteen years ahead of us. We are promised only today with hope for tomorrow.

Even on parole, we can't focus on the conditions that attempt to shackle us. Our parole conditions are a constant reminder of our past and an attempt to try to hold us back from progressing in society, but God! Every day, we have to shake the mental shackles that try to arrest us and hold us captive. We didn't just leave that abuse in prison; it was released with us - deeply embedded in our minds. We wrestle with mental battles every day and will have to deal with them for the rest of our lives. We think about the fact that we went to prison every day we wake up, but God!

It's a shame to think we had to go through all of that abuse for no reason at all. That in itself is a crime! We wish to God that we could just erase those thoughts from our brain. They aren't memories, they're nightmares–haunting nightmares. A simple thought about prison brings emotions that are overwhelming for us. It's a devastating way to live, but this is our life. We were released, but too often we mentally feel like we're still in prison. We can choose to incarcerate ourselves by being mentally imprisoned, or we can live in the freedom God gave us. We make a mental choice *every* day.

We are thankful for where we are in life, and we'll continue to press forward against all odds. The only way we can fail is if we stop. We run into obstacles every day, but we keep pressing on. We laugh when we hear someone say they're having a bad day. Oh really? We've got a bad day for you! We choose to look at our release as the beginning of a *new* life instead of the end of our prison sentence. We choose to believe that God didn't allow us to serve sixteen years in prison, be abused, release us, and not have more plans in store for our life. Not *our* God, and definitely not our Bigmama's God. Even if God's plan is for us to simply recognize the power He placed in us to press forward, it's a plan. We'll take that! We're not looking for some big pie-in-the-sky success story, because to survive sixteen years in prison and be alive to tell the story is success to us. Our hope is for progress in our life and to maintain a level of peace of mind.

With the few resources we have, we are making the best of our life on parole. Not only do we have the physical restrictions placed on us, but we have our own mental restrictions to deal with. To place young people in jail or prison, guilty or not, for extended periods of time with no formal rehabilitation or opportunity for educational growth besides obtaining a GED should be considered a crime. Inmates with extended prison sentences, such as ours, are not given the opportunity to take college courses. The system doesn't receive a payback because the chances of the inmate being released are slim to none. Therefore, the education the inmate receives would never be used. The system considers this a waste of money. Sounds crazy, but not getting our education taught us something. It taught us that an education is never a waste. Having knowledge is priceless, and not having it is imprisonment.

"You got the power. Strong minds break strong chains."

Omar Neal, former Mayor of Tuskegee, Alabama

If we were allowed to take some college classes while sitting in prison, we probably would have been able to keep our minds out of the gutter and the other dark places we visited. Instead, the system chose to keep us in the dark. There are so many young mothers and fathers in prison with no skills or education. Like us, these inmates will enter society and be responsible for raising and teaching their kids with an unstable foundation across the board – mentally, socially, academically, financially, and emotionally. This damaging cycle leaves a large part of society in a stagnated state of progression, which in turn affects society as a whole. Unless a strong family unit and community support is in-place when inmates are released, they are left to rehabilitate themselves, or go back to prison.

Seeds of defeat and failure are planted in the minds of inmates. It seems the system wants ex-offenders to return to prison, and many do. Over the sixteen years we spent in prison, we saw so many inmates return to prison over and over. It seemed like the same inmates were coming back and forth. It was ridiculous and we didn't understand why in the world they would come back. Prison was like a revolving door. Why? The returning inmates explained to us just how hard it was to make it "out there" with a felony charge on your record and have no support. When filling out a job application, ex-offenders know the application will end up in the trash once employers find out about past convictions.

A lot of inmates end up working for businesses that pay under the table or barely pay enough for you to get by. There are some merciful business owners and managers that will have a heart and look beyond an ex-offender's record, but they are few and far between. Most business owners are hesitant and don't want to take a chance. We've met some of those merciful business owners, and we've been through quite a few jobs. We will always be thankful for those employers who knew our past and still gave us a chance.

The truth is, not all inmates *want* to return to prison. Very

249

few inmates leave prison with a mission to fail and get locked up again. There are more inmates who want to be released and make an honest living than not, but they need support. They need someone to recognize their potential, but most employers look on the surface without going deep enough to see the ex-offender's desire and drive to make it in the world.

Gladys

Jamie and me lived together when we first got out of prison, but we later decided to get our own places. I went to a lot of apartment complexes tryin' to find a place to live. I was turned down by ten apartment managers 'cause of my record. I finally found a private owner that gave me a chance. I was so thankful. This is just one way showin' just how easy it is to end up back in prison. In order to get a job, you gotta have a address – shelters don't count. Everybody ain't as fortunate as I was to find a place to live. When ex-offenders don't have community or family support, or if no one will give 'em a chance to try to make it, they might turn to old ways to make a way for themselves and their family.

I refused to chase so-so jobs barely payin' minimum wage for the rest of my life. I worked for pennies, and sometimes free while I was in prison, but I ain't in prison no more. I was gettin' tired of workin' minimum wage jobs and barely makin' it. Workin' two jobs just to pay my few bills and eat ain't how I wanted to spend the rest of my life. I ain't afraid to work, and I'll do what I gotta do to make it. I want somebody to recognize me for the skills I got and for my work ethics rather than the convictions in my past – false convictions! I always felt like there was somethin' better for me. I just wanted the same opportunity the next person had to succeed. I did my time for the crime I did *not* commit, so I started prayin' for a good job.

Because of a "connection" someone in my life had, they was able to get me a job at a local law firm. This "connection" wasn't nothin' like the illegal connections Daddy had, but this connection was actually workin' for my good in a way nobody could get the credit for, but God. Talk about givin' ex-convicts a chance! At one time, I needed a lawyer, and I had always wanted to be a lawyer, but I never thought in a million years that I'd be workin' at a law firm. I thank God for *everybody* who gave me a chance. Those chances led me to where I am now. God knows I'm thankful because it ain't been easy.

~

We thank God for the compassionate people placed in our path to trust us and give us an opportunity to make it. Everybody deserves a chance to at least prove themselves. We made some mistakes in our early years. We had babies at an early age and dropped out of high school, but we both have our GED, and we are both employed.

Society looks at ex-offenders and automatically assumes they don't want to do anything with their lives. They judge us before they even talk to us. Of course, there are definitely those who get out of prison and fail, but thank God

251

that wasn't the case with us. Nobody knew how bad we wanted to make it in life. We didn't just want to survive, we wanted to thrive in our lives. It seems a little harder for us just because we're the "Scott Sisters," and it'll probably take us a lot longer than the average person, but we'll do what we have to do to make it. It doesn't matter if people doubt us. We don't have anything to prove to nobody except ourselves. We would love to prove to our kids that we can be good mothers, but right now we're proving to ourselves that we can make it in society.

Our brothers have been a strong force in our lives since we've been released. Mama and Daddy's lessons of being there for family were not in vain. We thank God for our siblings and the love and support they've shown us. Rat, who we felt alienated us while we were incarcerated, has visited us several times since we've been released. It took some time for us to reconnect, but we are so thankful we did. We've been able to rebuild our relationship with him, and we're closer than we've ever been. Rat has been there for us *and* Shamira. He stepped back in our lives just when we really needed a big brother. Rat is still serving in the United States Army and we're so proud of him. Rat has given us hope for the relationships we are trying to rebuild with our kids.

Call – Reclaim – Edify

Our first year out of prison was also edifying for us, and we don't use the word "edify" lightly. We didn't even know what the word meant, and really hadn't heard the word before, but we learned the word from the church we chose to fellowship with when we moved to Pensacola. "Edify" is a part of the church's mission statement. We thank the Greater Little Rock Baptist Church family for being a huge part of our community support. The mission statement of our church is: *Calling* sinners to repentance, *reclaiming* the backslider and *edifying* the Saints of God for the glory of God. Call, reclaim, and edify – we needed all three of these elements to help us get our life back on track.

Bible study in prison reminded us of Bigmama's faith, and reminded us to call on Bigmama's God, but to sit on a pew in church and have the freedom to worship without restrictions showed us how to get to know God for ourselves. The spiritual food and fellowship we received from this church helped us keep a positive attitude and maintain our hope and faith. We were beyond thankful to be introduced to this church.

Gladys

I was the first to fellowship and join the Greater Little Rock Church 'cause Jamie wanted to visit a few other churches before makin' her decision. After my first visit to the church, I knew where I belonged. I had been used and abused so much in my life that the love and support this church family showed me was amazin' to me. There was days in prison I didn't want to live, but hearin' God's word showed me there was another life for me – a life with Him. My past wasn't an issue with this church, but my future and gettin' me on the right track for my new life was. I didn't feel like they saw dollar signs when they saw me, and I didn't think they would exploit the "Scott Sisters" name for their own benefit. I was so happy when Jamie finally decided to join the GLR family. I was happy *and* relieved because I wanted us to fellowship together. We did everything else together, so why not go to church together?

I will never forget the first time I had communion with my new church family. We take communion together, seated, while Pastor Wesley stands in front of the congregation and shares the meanin', benefits, and the importance of the bread and wine. While Pastor Wesley spoke, I thought about how grateful I was for God keepin' me those sixteen hard years in prison. I thought about the years of abuse. I thought about my release. I thought about God's protection and mercy over my life and my kids' lives. I thought about Mama and everything she did to help us get released. I thought about being free from drugs.

I thought about so much and before I knew it, I stood up. I was so thankful, I had to stand to my feet to take my first communion. Somethin' wouldn't let me sit down. Thinkin' about Jesus and how he died for me when I was the one sentenced to die came over me in a way I can't explain. My emotions was messed up, and I couldn't handle what I was feelin'. Jesus was convicted of a crime He didn't commit. If nobody else understands that, me and Jamie do. I felt like I was standin' to give God honor and to recognize who He was in *my* life. I was the only one standin', but I didn't care. I didn't care about nobody else. I only saw myself as a child of God needin' the grace and mercy of her God. I love my God. I love my church and I love my pastor, too.

~

We believe *everything* we've been through was for a purpose. The prison system broke us, but God continues to mold us and make us. We were broken vessels, but God! Sure, it's easy to say this now that we're out of prison and looking back over our life, but hindsight has a powerful way of putting things in perspective. Being two peas in a pod on the streets of Chicago to being two peas in prison in Mississippi was life changing for us. We are now two peas in Pensacola using what we've been through to share a message of hope with someone who might be imprisoned by bars or imprisoned in their own mind.

Our hearts haven't been hardened by the unusual circumstances in our life, but we are driven by an intense compassion to help others. This passion leads us in so many different directions. We want to help whoever we can with the little resources we have. We're often asked to speak and share our story of hope to churches, schools, youth groups, and other organizations.

While we were in prison, we never thought anyone would want to hear anything about us. We were just two Mississippi sisters in prison. We were convicts that nobody seemed to care about. While we were looking out of our 15th floor bedroom window at everybody, it never crossed our mind that someone would want to read about our life. We weren't even supposed to have a life, but God!

If we can stop a child from going to prison, or help someone make better choices in life, we are doing our part. If we can offer hope to hurting, abused men and women, we are doing our part. We can't hold the hands of the youth and we aren't in any position to give instructions on how to live life, but we are here to share *our* journey and how God has been working in *our* life even when we weren't aware of His presence. We didn't see God working while we were in prison, and sometimes we didn't think He was working at all. We still have challenges to face, but we know God is with us. Actually, He never left us. Even if we can't see Him working, He's always working – we know this now.

God was with us for sixteen of the darkest years of our life, and He promised to be with us for the rest of our lives. We don't know what the future holds, but we live on the same mustard seed faith that we lived on in prison. We don't want to sound like we have a level of faith to brag about, because there are days that mustard seed seems to get smaller and smaller, but as long as it's still a seed, we'll be okay. As long as we remember God said He would never leave us, we're alright. Everything is alright.

"You either believe in God or you don't."

Georgia Blackmon, The Gathering Awareness & Book Center

Pensacola, FL

Jamie

While we were working on this book, I went through some real hard times. It seemed like nothing was going right. Every part of my life had something going on and there were mornings I didn't feel like getting out of bed. One morning, I woke up at 3 a.m. and I remembered how God used to wake me up in prison at 3 a.m. and I would get out of my rack and lay on the hard, cold, prison floor prostrate before God and pray.

When I start feeling sorry for myself, I remember those early mornings in prison. Sometimes I have to grab my Bible, read a few scriptures, and get on the floor like I did in prison and pray. Sometimes I call a friend to pray with me. Sometimes I just cry out to God for more strength to make it through the next hour. Some days I feel more broken than I was in prison and I beg for God's help and relief from all the pain in my life – all the pain in my body – all the pain in my mind. I feel so much better when I recognize that my pain is real instead of acting like it doesn't exist. Prayer has never failed me. Even when my faith waivered, I kept praying.

~

We were wrongly convicted, abused and scarred. We're on parole for life. We have a felony record. We have kids who don't know us. We have nightmares about prison. We've got sixteen years of baggage and we don't know what tomorrow holds, but God! We have to hold on to our faith for better days.

While writing this book, the woman that gave us life and

fought for our freedom, Mama, passed away. Mama gave all her time and energy to fight for our freedom. She basically gave her life to give us our lives back. We miss Mama, and our hearts hurt for her every day. Not a day goes by that we don't think about how she fought so hard for our freedom. We wish she was still here to help us fight for our pardon, but she made it clear that we would have to fight to get off parole ourselves. Mama fought her whole life, and we are at peace knowing she is at peace. She knew we were writing this book, and although she didn't get to see the finished product, she finished what she set out to do, and that was to make sure we were free. Now, Mama is free.

Both of our parents did the best they could. They had children to use drugs, join gangs, and even go to prison, but we believe with all our heart that they loved us. Yes, things could have been different, but our goal is to look forward and strive to live our best life – even on parole. We still have a lot of challenges and many obstacles ahead of us, but God!

We were each other's strength while we were in prison. Today is a brand new day! Since our release from prison, we have been strong advocates for people who have been wrongly accused and convicted. We both have struggled to move on and work hard at a normal life where we are not defined by our past. Jamie is also continuing her education and has enrolled at Pensacola State, majoring in business. We take each day as it comes and continue to allow God to lead our path to true happiness.

1   A.   Uh-huh.

2   Q.   I'm sorry?

3   A.   Yes.

4   Q.   Who told you that?

5   A.   My lawyer.

6   Q.   And, did you give a statement concerning this matter?

7   A.   Yes.

8   Q.   Did you write it out in your own handwriting?

9   A.   Yes.

0   Q.   You did?

1   A.   Yes.

2   Q.   Is this the statement that you gave?

3   A.   (Examining) Yes.

4   Q.   And, this is your handwriting?

5   A.   Uh-huh.

6   Q.   I'm sorry?

7   A.   Yes.

8   Q.   It is?

9   A.   Yes.

0   Q.   Okay. Who was present when you gave this statement?

1   A.   Marvin Williams and Jerry McNeece.

2   Q.   Did you have a lawyer present?

3   A.   No, I did not.

4   Q.   Why didn't you have a lawyer present?

5   A.   I don't know.

6   Q.   You don't know? Could you afford to have a lawyer

7 present?

8   A.   No.

9   Q.   You could not?

INDEX

Excerpts from Court Tran

Witness Statement

Affidavit

Verdict

1   A.   N

2   Q.   Did you ask to have anyone else present, besides these

3 law enforcement officers?

4   A.   Say that again.

5   Q.   Did you ask to have anyone else present besides them?

6   A.   No.

7   Q.   Why not?

8   A.   I don't know.

9   BY MR. TURNER: Object to the relevancy, Your Honor.

10   BY THE COURT: Sustained.

11   Q.   (Alexander) Mr. Patrick, you have testified that you

12 followed the car, you were in a car that followed another car?

13   A.   Uh-huh.

14   Q.   To Hillsboro?

15   A.   Yes.

16   Q.   And, that after you got to Hillsboro, you and you

17 brother --

18   A.   My cousins.

19   Q.   You and your two cousins?

20   A.   Uh-huh.

21   Q.   Got out of the car and robbed two men?

22   A.   Yeah.

23   Q.   Is that right?

24   A.   Yeah.

25   Q.   Okay; and, all three of you, all three of you,

26 participated in the robbery; is that right?

27   A.   Yes.

28   Q.   Now, so that means all three of you were out of the car?

29   A.   Yes.

```
1        Q.   :  that right?                                      ...
2        A.   Yes.
3        Q.   Who was driving the car that was in front of you aft
4    you left the Cow Pasture?
5        A.   After we left the Cow Pasture?
6        Q.   Yes.
7        A.   Gladys.
8        Q.   Well, did you write in your statement that Jamie was
9    driving the car?
10       A.   I don't believe so.
11            BY MR. ALEXANDER: May I approach the witness, Your
12            Honor?
13            BY THE COURT: Yes.
14       Q.   (Alexander)  See that right there?  "Jamie was driving
15   the car."
16       A.   Uh-huh.
17       Q.   "After we left the club."
18       A.   Yeah.
19       Q.   Well, who was driving the car?
20       A.   Gladys.
21       Q.   Well, why did you write "Jamie"?
22       A.   That ain't my handwriting.
23       Q.   Well, I thought you said it was your handwriting?
24       A.   That's a different one.
25       Q.   I'm sorry?
26       A.   That's a different statement.
27       Q.   This is a different statement than the one you gave?
28       A.   That's not my handwriting right there.
29       Q.   Okay.  Do you remember a few minutes ago I asked you .
```

263

1   this was your handwriting?

2   A.   Yeah. I know my handwriting, too.

3   Q.   You remember I asked you that question?

4   A.   Yeah.

5   Q.   Do you remember telling me that it was your handwriting?

6   A.   Yes.

7   Q.   Okay; but, now you are telling me that it is not your

8   handwriting?

9   A.   It ain't.

10   Q.   Okay. Then when did you tell me before that it was?

11   A.   Because that's a different page.

12   Q.   But, why did you tell me -- this is a different page? Is

13 that what you are saying?

14   A.   Uh-huh.

15   Q.   This is a different page from what I showed you before?

16   A.   That's not my handwriting.

17   Q.   Okay. Well, let me show you all of it. Which is your

18 handwriting, and which is not?

19   A.   (Examining) That's my handwriting.

20   Q.   This is your handwriting here?

21   A.   Yeah.

22   Q.   But, this is not?

23   A.   No, it is not.

24   Q.   Okay. Who wrote this?

25   A.   I don't know.

26   Q.   You don't know?

27   A.   No, I don't.

28   Q.   Was this written before you signed it?

29   BY MR. TURNER: Objection, Your Honor. He didn't

1   sign it.

2   Q.   (Alexander) You didn't sign this?

3   A.   Sign what?

4   Q.   This page?

5   A.   No.

6   Q.   I'm sorry?

7   A.   No, I didn't sign that page.

8   Q.   You didn't sign this page, and what's on here is not what

9   you told the officers?

10   A.   I might have told them, but I didn't sign that.

11   Q.   Well, did you tell them that Jamie was driving the car?

12   A.   No, I did not.

13   Q.   Okay. So, whoever wrote this was writing it down wrong?

14   A.   I guess they was.

15   Q.   Well, who was writing it?

16   A.   I don't know.

17   Q.   Who was present when you talked to the officers?

18   A.   Nobody.

19   Q.   You didn't talk to the officers?

20   A.   Yes, I did.

21   Q.   Who were the officers who were present?

22   A.   Jerry McNeece and Marvin Williams.

23   Q.   So, you signed one page?

24   A.   Yes, I did.

25   Q.   Okay; and, that page that you signed is in your

26   handwriting?

27   A.   Yes, it is.

28   (PAUSE IN PROCEEDINGS)

29   Q.   (Alexander) The statement that you signed is this page?

265

1   A.   I.o, it is.

2   Q.   And, this is the statement that\you wrote?

3   A.   Yes, it is.

4   Q.   Is that right?

5   A.   Yes.

6   Q.   This statement does not say that Jamie Scott and Gladys

7 Scott got in the car with you and Chris and Gregory. Who is the

8 other one? Howard. Is that right?

9   A.   What?

10   Q.   The statement that you wrote and you signed does not say

11 that Jamie Scott and Gladys Scott got in the car with you aft'

12 these guys were robbed. Isn't that true?

13   A.   I don't know.

14   Q.   Well, read it.

15   A.   I think it do.

16   Q.   Read it.

17   A.   (Examining) "I give this statement --

18   Q.   I didn't ask you to read it aloud. Read it to yourself.

19   A.   All right. (Reading)

20   Q.   So, am I correct?

21   A.   Yes.

22   Q.   It doesn't say that; does it?

23   A.   Unh-unh.

24   Q.   Does it?

25   A.   No.

26   Q.   It doesn't say that they got in the car with you all and

27 left; does it? Does it?

28   BY MR. TURNER: Your Honor, I will object. It ha

29   been asked and answered.

```
1              BY MR. ALEXANDER:   I just want to be sure it's
2      clear.
3              BY THE COURT:   Go ahead and answer the question.
4      A.   No.
5      Q.   (Alexander)  It doesn't say that; does it?
6      A.   No.
7      Q.   And, the other statement you didn't write?
8      A.   Unh-unh.
9      Q.   Didn't read?
10     A.   Unh-unh.
11     Q.   Is that right?
12     A.   No, I didn't write it.
13     Q.   And, you don't even know who wrote it?  Right?
14     A.   That's right.
15     Q.   Okay.
16             BY MR. ALEXANDER:  If you will indulge me, I'm just
17     about to conclude, Your Honor.
18                 (PAUSE IN PROCEEDINGS)
19     Q.   (Alexander)  Let me make sure I'm clear once more.  This
20  page right here is the page that you wrote?
21     A.   (Examining)  Uh-huh.
22     Q.   Correct?
23     A.   Yes.
24     Q.   Okay; and, that page is about three-quarters of a legal
25  size page long?
26     A.   Yeah.
27     Q.   Correct?
28     A.   Yeah.
29     Q.   Who was present while you were writing that?
```

267

1   A.   J : me and the officers.

2   Q.   Those two officers?

3   A.   (No answer)

4   Q.   Did they tell you to write it out in your own

5 handwriting?

6   A.   Yes.

7   Q.   Okay. Were they asking you questions while you were

8 writing it?

9   A.   Yes, they was.

10   Q.   Now, I notice that throughout the first three-quarters of

11 the page that you wrote, you did not indicate in any respect tha'

12 Gladys Scott or Jamie Scott had anything to do with the robbery.

13 Isn't that true?

14   A.   Uh-huh.

15   Q.   Okay; but, at the very end you added something that was

16 out of sequence to the other information that you had written. L

17 you recall that?

18   A.   Unh-unh.

19   Q.   Something about what they had told you. Do you

20 understand what I am asking you?

21   A.   Unh-unh.

22   Q.   Now, in the statement that you wrote, in that statement,

23 it never said anything about Gladys holding any guns; did it?

24   A.   No.

25   Q.   Beg your pardon?

26   A.   No.

27   Q.   And, it didn't say anything about y'all driving off

28 together; did it?

29   A.   No.

1   Q.   W : it did say was that Chr. got out of the car to go

2   and talk to the guys in the other car about trying to touch Jamie.

3   Isn't that what it says?

4   A.   Uh-huh.

5   Q.   Well, was that true or not?

6   A.   Yeah, it's true.

7   Q.   That's why Chris got out of the car?

8   A.   What you saying?

9   Q.   Is that why Chris got out of the car?

10 A.   No, we got out of the car to see what was going on.

11 Q.   You got out of the car to see what was going on. Wha-

12 you say you got out of the car, you are talking about out at

13 Hillsboro; is that right?

14 A.   Out at Hillsboro? No, on the scene.

15 Q.   I'm sorry?

16 A.   On the scene.

17 Q.   What scene?

18 A.   The scene of the crime.

19 Q.   The scene of the crime, is that what you are saying?

20 A.   Yes.

21 Q.   Okay. You got out at the scene of the crime to see what

22 was going on. Is that your testimony? Is that what you just said?

23 A.   To see what was going on while they was fighting, or

24 whatever they was doing.

25 Q.   While they were fighting? Who was fighting?

26 A.   Her and the dude in the backseat.

27 Q.   Who and the dude in the backseat?

28 A.   Jamie.

29 Q.   Jamie was fighting with a dude in the backseat; is tha

1   right?

2   A.   Yes.

3   Q.   And, you all stopped your car to see why they w

4   fighting?

5   A.   Yes.

6   Q.   Is that right?

7   A.   Yes.

8   Q.   Because you could see that they were fighting from where

9   you were?

10   A.   Yeah.

11   (PAUSE IN PROCEEDINGS)

12   BY MR. ALEXANDER: No further questions, Your Honor.

13   BY THE COURT: Redirect?

14   REDIRECT EXAMINATION BY MR. TURNER:

15   Q.   Gregory?

16   A.   Yes, sir.

17   Q.   So, I can clear this up, the first piece of paper that

18   Mr. Alexander showed you, is this the one he asked you if this was

19   in your handwriting?

20   A.   (Examining) Yeah.

21   Q.   And, is that your handwriting?

22   A.   Yes, that's my handwriting.

23   Q.   Now, the second one he showed you, this is not the same

24   one he showed you the first time; is that correct?

25   A.   Yeah.

26   Q.   Is this the same or different from this page?

27   A.   Different.

28   Q.   All right. Now, this is not your handwriting; is that

29   A.   No, sir.

270

1   Q.   -- correct? All right. In addition to writing this

2   statement down here, did you have occasion to talk to Jerry McNeece

3   and Marvin Williams about what happened?

4   A.   Yes.

5   Q.   And, do you know whether or not they were writing down

6   what you were saying?

7   A.   No.

8   Q.   You don't know?

9   A.   They wasn't.

10   Q.   Okay. Could you tell me whether or not you told them

11 that after the men were robbed, that Jamie and Gladys got in th

12 car with y'all?

13   A.   Yes.

14   Q.   Did you tell them that?

15   A.   Yes, I did.

16   Q.   All right. You weren't purporting to say that this pape

17 here, whatever it may be, was something that you had signed or

18 anything; is that correct?

19   A.   That's correct.

20   Q.   All right. When we are talking about your statement,

21 this is the one you signed here?

22   A.   That is correct.

23   Q.   Okay. At any point in time, Gregory, did anyone tell you

24 in order for your plea-bargaining to go through, you had to d

25 anything other than tell the truth?

26   A.   No.

27   Q.   Did anyone try to put words in your mouth about what to

28 say about Jamie or Gladys?

29   A.   No, they did not.

134

1   Q. A right.

2   BY MR. TURNER: I believe that's all, Your Honor.

3   BY THE COURT: You can go back to the witness roo

4   (WITNESS EXCUSED)

5   BY THE COURT: Ladies and gentlemen, it's twenty

6   minutes until 5:00 o'clock. We are going to recess for

7   the remainder of the day. While you are in recess,

8   again, you will be instructed not to discuss this among

9   yourselves, or with anyone else. If anyone should

10   attempt to talk to you, give me that person's name and

11   tell me what that person had to say. Do not have a

12   conversation at all with the attorneys or the parties or

13   this case or any of the witnesses.

14   All persons will remain seated. I will let the jury

15   pass through this door here. You are recessed until 9:00

16   o'clock tomorrow morning.

17   WHEREUPON, AT 4:40 P.M., THESE PROCEEDINGS WERE CONCLUDED FOR

18   THE DAY. AT 9:15 A.M., TUESDAY, OCTOBER 4, 1994, THE JUDGE, COURT

19   REPORTER, AND ALL ATTORNEYS RETIRED TO CHAMBERS, THE PRESENCE OF

20   THE DEFENDANTS BEING WAIVED, AND THE FOLLOWING PROCEEDINGS WERE HAD

21   OUT OF THE PRESENCE OF THE JURY:

22   BY THE COURT: It is now fifteen minutes past 9:00 o'clock,

23   and the juror, Lilly Massey, has not appeared. I've been waiting

24   this time for her to show. I've had the Clerk to attempt to ca'

25   her, but she has no telephone, so we have no information as to why

26   she is not here.

27   I propose to continue with the trial of the case and to seat

28   the first alternate, George Moore, Jr., in her stead.

29   Are you all in opposition to that?

Verdict   174

1   BY THE COURT: Mr. Stacy Weger, the Court has a need for
2   someone to conduct the conversations of the jury and serve as the
3   spokesman between the jury and the Court.

4   Whenever you go to the jury room, from among yourselves you
5   select that person.

6   Now, the clerk will furnish you the matters that have been
7   introduced into evidence as exhibits, the jury instructions, and
8   clean sheets of paper.

9   There's two instructions that has the forms of the verdicts
10 that can be returned in this case. All twelve of you must agree to
11 the verdict that is returned.

12 You must return separate verdicts for these two Defendants, a
13 verdict for each Defendant. In the event all twelve of you do
14 agree, you write your verdict on a separate sheet of paper, with no
15 writing on that separate sheet of paper, other than the verdict
16 the jury.

17 Announce to the Bailiffs that you have arrived at a verdict,
18 remain there in the jury room, and I will send for you.

19 Would you please, Mr. Weger, come around and receive these
20 matters from the Clerk?

21 I am going to let the jury, please, be retired with the
22 Bailiffs.

23 WHEREUPON, AT 11:35 A.M., THE JURY WAS RETIRED TO THE JURY
24 ROOM TO DELIBERATE ITS VERDICTS. AT 12:11 P.M., WITH THE
25 DEFENDANTS AND ALL ATTORNEYS PRESENT IN THE COURTROOM, THE JURY WAS
26 RETURNED TO THE COURTROOM, IN FRONT OF THE BENCH, AND THE FOLLOWING
27 PROCEEDINGS WERE HAD IN THE PRESENCE OF THE JURY:

28 BY THE COURT: Let the record show all twelve jurors are in
29 the Courtroom in the presence of the Defendants and the attorneys

273

Verdict   175

1   on this, a regular day of this term.

2   It was announced to me that the jury had reached a verdict.

3   Mr. Weger, is my information correct? Are you the spokesman for

4   the jury?

5   BY JUROR WEGER: Yes, sir.

6   BY THE COURT: Is my information correct, the jury has reached

7   a verdict?

8   BY JUROR WEGER: Yes, sir.

9   BY THE COURT: Have you reached a verdict regarding both

10 Defendants?

11   BY JUROR WEGER: Yes, sir.

12   BY THE COURT: And, is the verdict regarding both Defendants

13 a unanimous verdict?

14   BY JUROR WEGER: Yes, sir.

15   BY THE COURT: May I see the verdicts, please?

16   (JUDGE EXAMINES VERDICTS)

17   BY THE COURT: The two verdicts that were handed me, did you

18 agree to both of them?

19   BY JUROR WEGER: Yes, sir.

20   (JURY IS POLLED)

21   BY THE COURT: Do not file the verdicts, but read both

22 verdicts.

23   BY THE CIRCUIT CLERK: "We, the jury, find the Defendants,

24 Gladys Scott and Jamie Scott, guilty as charged in Count I and

25 unanimously agree to fix their punishment at imprisonment for

26 life."

27   "We, the jury, find the Defendants, Gladys Scott and Jamie

28 Scott, guilty as charged in Count II and unanimously agree to fix

29 their punishment at imprisonment for life."

1   BY THE COURT: Mr. Alexander, would you like the jury again to

2 be polled?

3   BY MR. ALEXANDER: Yes, sir.

4   BY THE COURT: The verdicts that were read by the Clerk, did

5 you agree to both of those verdicts?

6   BY JUROR WEGER: Yes, sir.

7   (JURY IS POLLED)

8   BY THE COURT: Upon again being polled, all twelve jurors

9 indicated that they agreed to both verdicts as read by the Clerk.

10   Ladies and gentlemen, I am going to let you be recessed for

11 the remainder of the day. You call in after 5:00 o'clock this

12 afternoon for instructions when to return.

13   You may pass through this door.

14   (JURORS ARE EXCUSED AND EXIT THE COURTROOM)

15   BY THE COURT: Let both Defendants please stand. Do you have

16 any reason, anything to say, why sentence should not be pronounced

17 at this time?

18   BY MR. ALEXANDER: No, Your Honor.

19   BY THE COURT: Do you, Ms. Pierson?

20   BY MS. PIERSON: No, Your Honor.

21   BY THE COURT: Gladys Scott, Jamie Scott, you both have been

22 found guilty as charged. The jury had the option of sentencing you

23 to life imprisonment for the crime of armed robbery. They have

24 elected to sentence you to life imprisonment.

25   Therefore, Gladys Scott, it is the sentence of this Court that

26 you serve life imprisonment in Count I of the indictment. In Count

27 II of the indictment, it's the sentence of this Court that you

28 serve life imprisonment, with this sentence to run consecutive to

29 the sentence pronounced upon you in Count I.

1   Jamie Scott, it is the sentence of this Court in Count I of

2   the indictment that you serve life imprisonment, and in Count II of

3   the indictment, it is the sentence of this Court that you ser

4   life imprisonment, with this sentence to run consecutive to the

5   sentence pronounced upon you in Count I.

6   Both of you are committed to the custody of the Sheriff of

7   this county.

8   Court is in recess until 1:00 o'clock.

9   WHEREUPON, THESE PROCEEDINGS WERE CONCLUDED FOR THE DAY. ON

10   THURSDAY, OCTOBER 13, 1994, THE JUDGE, COURT REPORTER, MR. TURNER,

11   MR. DUNCAN, MR. ALEXANDER, AND MS. PIERSON RETIRED TO CHAMBERS, THE

12   PRESENCE OF THE DEFENDANTS BEING WAIVED, AND THE FOLLOWING

13   PROCEEDINGS WERE HAD:

14   BY THE COURT: For the record, Mr. Alexander has requested the

15   District Attorney to acknowledge his failure to provide a written

16   statement that he has no criminal record of the witness.

17   BY MR. ALEXANDER: Your Honor, it was several witnesses they

18   never provided us any documentation for. The District Attorney,

19   despite the motion submitted by the defense, never provided any

20   written documentation of any criminal histories of any of the

21   witnesses who testified on behalf of the State or listed as

22   possible witnesses on behalf of the State.

23   In the trial, one of the complaining witnesses was currently

24   incarcerated in the Simpson County Jail, and his appearance had

25   been procured by the District Attorney, but that fact was not made

26   known to the defense prior to the morning of the trial, and the

27   defense was left with only the testimony and claims of the witness

28   as to his criminal history, and to this date, defense counsel i

29   unaware of the actual criminal histories of the witnesses offered